59705

W9-BZB-611

Opposing Viewpoints®

Male/Female Roles

Opposing Viewpoints ®

Male/Female Roles

Other Books of Related Interest

Opposing Viewpoints ®

Male/Female Roles

Auriana Ojeda, *Book Editor*

Bruce Glassman, *Vice President*
Bonnie Szumski, *Publisher*
Helen Cothran, *Managing Editor*

OPPOSING
VIEWPOINTS®
SERIES

GREENHAVEN PRESS
An imprint of Thomson Gale, a part of The Thomson Corporation

THOMSON
™
GALE

Detroit • New York • San Francisco • San Diego • New Haven, Conn.
Waterville, Maine • London • Munich

For more information, contact
Greenhaven Press
27500 Drake Rd.
Farmington Hills, MI 48331-3535
Or you can visit our Internet site at http://www.gale.com

Cover credit: © PhotoDisc

LIBRARY OF CONGRESS CATALOGING-IN-PUBLICATION DATA

Male/female roles : opposing viewpoints / Auriana Ojeda, book editor.
   p. cm. — (Opposing viewpoints series)
Includes bibliographical references and index.
ISBN 0-7377-2240-1 (lib. bdg. : alk. paper) —
ISBN 0-7377-2241-X (pbk. : alk. paper)
   1. Sex roles. 2. Masculinity. 3. Feminism. 4. Sexism. 5. Man-woman relationships.
I. Ojeda, Auriana, 1977– . II. Opposing viewpoints series (Unnumbered)
HQ1075.M35 2005
305.3—dc22   2004040605

Printed in the United States of America

"Congress shall make
no law...abridging the
freedom of speech, or of
the press."

First Amendment to the U.S. Constitution

The basic foundation of our democracy is the First
Amendment guarantee of freedom of expression.
The Opposing Viewpoints Series is dedicated to the
concept of this basic freedom and the idea that it is
more important to practice it than to enshrine it.

Contents

Why Consider Opposing Viewpoints?

*"The only way in which a human being can make some
approach to knowing the whole of a subject is by hearing
what can be said about it by persons of every variety of
opinion and studying all modes in which it can be looked
at by every character of mind. No wise man ever
acquired his wisdom in any mode but this."*

John Stuart Mill

In our media-intensive culture it is not difficult to find differing opinions. Thousands of newspapers and magazines
and dozens of radio and television talk shows resound with
differing points of view. The difficulty lies in deciding which
opinion to agree with and which "experts" seem the most
credible. The more inundated we become with differing
opinions and claims, the more essential it is to hone critical
reading and thinking skills to evaluate these ideas. Opposing
Viewpoints books address this problem directly by presenting stimulating debates that can be used to enhance and
teach these skills. The varied opinions contained in each
book examine many different aspects of a single issue. While
examining these conveniently edited opposing views, readers
can develop critical thinking skills such as the ability to
compare and contrast authors' credibility, facts, argumenta-
tion styles, use of persuasive techniques, and other stylistic
tools. In short, the Opposing Viewpoints Series is an ideal
way to attain the higher-level thinking and reading skills so
essential in a culture of diverse and contradictory opinions.

In addition to providing a tool for critical thinking, Opposing Viewpoints books challenge readers to question their
own strongly held opinions and assumptions. Most people
form their opinions on the basis of upbringing, peer pressure, and personal, cultural, or professional bias. By reading
carefully balanced opposing views, readers must directly
confront new ideas as well as the opinions of those with
whom they disagree. This is not to simplistically argue that

everyone who reads opposing views will—or should—change his or her opinion. Instead, the series enhances readers' understanding of their own views by encouraging confrontation with opposing ideas. Careful examination of others' views can lead to the readers' understanding of the logical inconsistencies in their own opinions, perspective on why they hold an opinion, and the consideration of the possibility that their opinion requires further evaluation.

Evaluating Other Opinions

To ensure that this type of examination occurs, Opposing Viewpoints books present all types of opinions. Prominent spokespeople on different sides of each issue as well as well-known professionals from many disciplines challenge the reader. An additional goal of the series is to provide a forum for other, less known, or even unpopular viewpoints. The opinion of an ordinary person who has had to make the decision to cut off life support from a terminally ill relative, for example, may be just as valuable and provide just as much insight as a medical ethicist's professional opinion. The editors have two additional purposes in including these less known views. One, the editors encourage readers to respect others' opinions—even when not enhanced by professional credibility. It is only by reading or listening to and objectively evaluating others' ideas that one can determine whether they are worthy of consideration. Two, the inclusion of such viewpoints encourages the important critical thinking skill of objectively evaluating an author's credentials and bias. This evaluation will illuminate an author's reasons for taking a particular stance on an issue and will aid in readers' evaluation of the author's ideas.

It is our hope that these books will give readers a deeper understanding of the issues debated and an appreciation of the complexity of even seemingly simple issues when good and honest people disagree. This awareness is particularly important in a democratic society such as ours in which people enter into public debate to determine the common good. Those with whom one disagrees should not be regarded as enemies but rather as people whose views deserve careful examination and may shed light on one's own.

Thomas Jefferson once said that "difference of opinion leads to inquiry, and inquiry to truth." Jefferson, a broadly educated man, argued that "if a nation expects to be ignorant and free . . . it expects what never was and never will be." As individuals and as a nation, it is imperative that we consider the opinions of others and examine them with skill and discernment. The Opposing Viewpoints Series is intended to help readers achieve this goal.

David L. Bender and Bruno Leone,
Founders

Greenhaven Press anthologies primarily consist of previously published material taken from a variety of sources, including periodicals, books, scholarly journals, newspapers, government documents, and position papers from private and public organizations. These original sources are often edited for length and to ensure their accessibility for a young adult audience. The anthology editors also change the original titles of these works in order to clearly present the main thesis of each viewpoint and to explicitly indicate the opinion presented in the viewpoint. These alterations are made in consideration of both the reading and comprehension levels of a young adult audience. Every effort is made to ensure that Greenhaven Press accurately reflects the original intent of the authors included in this anthology.

Introduction

"The 'loner profile' of testosterone is absolutely crucial to understanding what men are all about. . . . Testosterone motivates the male to strive for separateness in ways a woman is not designed to comprehend."
—Theresa Crenshaw, author of Sexual Pharmacology

"For women the absence of emotional support in the community increased their death rates more than eightfold. For men it made no difference at all."
—Steven E. Rhoads, professor of government at the University of Virginia

More than two hundred years ago, early feminist Mary Wollstonecraft wrote a treatise entitled "Vindication of the Rights of Woman" in which she argued that men and women are essentially the same. She suggested that the roles played by the two sexes are largely constructed by society. Since the treatise's publication, fierce debate has pitted social constructionists such as Wollstonecraft against essentialists, who argue that the differences between the sexes are biologically determined. Many people involved in this debate contend that deciding who is right could have an enormous impact on male/female relations.

Essentialists argue that gender differences are encoded in the brain and in the body's chemistry. Many essentialists claim that brain structure accounts for most of the differences between men and women. Neuroscientists have discovered, for example, that women's brains have a larger corpus callosum, which carries messages between the right and left hemispheres. Because the emotional right hemisphere and the verbal left hemisphere in women's brains can communicate more easily than in men's, women are generally more intuitive and better at expressing their emotions.

In addition to brain differences, many essentialist theorists argue that hormones play a large part in explaining the disparities between men and women. Testosterone, the primary male hormone, floods a boy's body at puberty and induces the growth of body hair, the deepening of the voice, and the development of muscles. Testosterone is also responsible for aggressiveness, sexual desire, and competitiveness. Both men and women produce testosterone, but women produce about 70 percent less than men. Thus, according to journalist Iain Murray, "Testosterone is crucial in making men men—literally."

Similarly, women produce a large quantity of a hormone called oxytocin, which promotes bonding and affiliation. According to researchers, both men and women produce oxytocin, but women produce it in greater quantities. Moreover, researchers contend that testosterone counteracts the effect of oxytocin, while estrogen, the primary female hormone, enhances it. Oxytocin promotes affection within relationships, but it is most known for enhancing the maternal instinct. Scientists maintain that oxytocin is released during childbirth and breastfeeding and is responsible for creating a strong bond between mother and child. The fact that women are more affected by oxytocin than men, according to experts, helps explains why women are often better nurturers and caretakers than are men.

Other experts dispute the theory that gender differences are attributable to biology. These experts contend that culture shapes roles for men and women, and they argue that children are born into societies that have preexisting gender norms and expectations. According to this view, known as social constructionism, boys and girls are socially conditioned to adopt gender-specific behaviors that society considers appropriate. Family, peers, and the media constantly reinforce these stereotypes. According to law professor Deborah L. Rhode,

> Whatever children's predispositions, they also receive frequent signals from parents, peers, teachers, and the media. In countless ways, our culture encourages boys to be assertive, competitive, and independent—to make things work and happen. We tell girls to be nice, caring, and dependent—to worry about how they look and what others feel. Females learn how to get along; males learn how to get ahead. And children of both sexes learn, above all, that gender matters.

The social cues that help construct gender, these analysts

claim, are present from the beginning of children's lives. For example, many parents decorate their babies' rooms in gender-specific wallpaper, such as adventure-theme paper depicting planes for boys and passive themes such as daisies for girls. Some studies have indicated that adults handle female and male infants differently. Boys are jiggled more whereas girls are coddled, and adults typically support a female infant's head more than a boy's. Even as infants, boys are considered sturdier than girls. These disparate treatments do not stop at infancy. Parents continue to treat boys differently from girls, many experts argue, as evidenced by the different chores assigned to children. Boys are often required to perform chores outside, such as mowing the lawn, whereas girls are usually asked to help inside with the cooking and cleaning. Many experts point out that children learn most of what they know about gender expectations by watching role models, usually their parents, who are most likely modeling dichotomous gender roles at home.

Although many people remain untroubled by traditional gender roles and see no need to question their origins, others argue that accepted gender roles must be reexamined, and that to do so requires an understanding of how gender identity is formed. Many of these analysts assert that gender dichotomy strains relations between the sexes. Author John Gray describes the emotional gulf between men and women in the title of his popular book, *Men Are from Mars, Women Are from Venus*. Journalist Anna Quindlen, in her essay "Between the Sexes, a Great Divide," visualizes this difference as the empty space on a dance floor, where boys stand on one side and girls on the other, each group afraid to talk to the other. Quindlen notes that a friend once articulated a similar conception by exclaiming, "I swear to God we are different species." The popular saying, "men and women simply speak a different language," suggests that many people perceive gender dichotomy as a barrier to understanding between the sexes. Indeed, women report being frustrated by what they perceive as men's linear thinking, their inattention to household chores, and their emotional distance. Men complain that women nag them about chores and smother them emotionally.

In the eyes of many, traditional gender roles lead to discord between the sexes. For this and other reasons, determining where notions of gender come from has become the subject of intense debate. The authors in *Male/Female Roles: Opposing Viewpoints* address this and other issues relating to gender in the following chapters: How Are Gender Roles Established? What Roles Should Women Embrace? What Should Men's Roles in Society Be? How Can Male/Female Relations Be Improved? Whether biologically determined or socially constructed, gender unquestionably shapes interactions between men and women, for better or ill.

CHAPTER 1

How Are Gender Roles Established?

Chapter Preface

English professor Michael Green grew increasingly frustrated at his inability to draw out his female students, who remained distressingly silent during class discussions. He had always believed that the best way to develop students' critical thinking skills was to ask for oral comments on particular topics and then challenge the students' arguments. The professor's male students had always appeared comfortable with this format, willingly sharing their opinions in class and seeming to view the professor's challenges as opportunities to learn. However, this approach clearly discouraged his female students from contributing. To try to solve the problem, Green decided to begin discussions by asking an open-ended question and letting all answers go unchallenged. To his surprise and delight, the women in his class began to speak up.

What accounts for the distinct gender behaviors Green saw in his classroom is the subject of heated debate. Some observers argue that these disparate behaviors are due to the biological differences between males and females. Because males' bodies make more of the hormone testosterone, these commentators claim that male students are naturally more aggressive and comfortable with being challenged. Other analysts disagree, claiming that the dissimilarities have roots in the environment, where boys are taught to be assertive and gifts to be passive. What most commentators do agree on is that girls and boys are simply different when they enter the school system, and, for better or worse, the educational system reinforces those differences.

Many analysts assert that America's educational system, because it was originally established by males for males, tends to reward and reinforce male behavior. Walter Ong, in his book *Fighting for Life*, contends that U.S. schools are based on ritual opposition, where public display is followed by argument and challenge (recall professor Green). Ong calls this type of classroom setting "adversativeness" or "agonism." Such a setting suits boys' learning styles but not girls', claims Deborah Tannen, who teaches linguistics at Georgetown University. According to Tannen, "Speaking in a classroom is more congenial to boys' language experience than to girls'" because "girls and boys learn to use language differently in their sex-separate peer groups." Girls typically have one or two best friends with whom they sit and talk, often sharing secrets. Boys, on the other hand, tend to play in larger groups, where members vie for dominance.

These different conversational styles, already in place when children enter school, can cause problems in classroom settings. Boys, who are used to taking center stage and responding to challenges, fare well in America's "adversative" school environment, according to some analysts. However, girls, who have little experience asserting themselves in large groups, do less well. Many commentators argue that girls' discomfort with classroom dynamics often develops into a lack of confidence in academic ability. Moreover, teachers often read girls' reticence to speak as a sign of academic deficiency, and they often find it easy to ignore these quiet female students. Thus, the gender differences apparent when children enter school become more pronounced as education continues: Boys become more assertive, girls quieter. Boys gain confidence in their academic abilities while girls lose confidence. Boys gravitate toward "hard" subjects such as science and math, where absolute answers are required, whereas girls are drawn toward "soft" subjects such as English, where many interpretations are considered valid.

What contributes to girls' and boys' different conversational styles and educational experiences remains controversial. The authors in the following chapter continue this discussion on what factors shape gender. As Michael Green's experience illustrates, the formation of gender identity is often the result of many factors interacting with one another.

"The difference [between men and women] is fundamental, encoded within us."

Biological Differences Establish Gender Roles

Geoffrey Norman

In the following viewpoint Geoffrey Norman argues that the differences between men and women are rooted in human biology. He contends that boys consistently choose to play with trucks and weapons while girls opt for dolls. According to Norman, men are aggressive and hierarchical while women are nurturing and cooperative. Although he enjoyed raising his daughters, Norman maintains that raising a son would have been a completely different experience. Geoffrey Norman writes for *Men's Health*, the *National Review*, and other publications.

As you read, consider the following questions:
1. What kind of toys did Norman buy for his children?
2. What difference between girls and boys did the author notice while fishing?
3. According to Norman, what authoritative behaviors do boys and girls respond to?

On one of those autumn days that God designed to break your heart, I was straddling an 8-by-8 beam about 15 feet off the ground. Three dozen of us were raising a house; it was serious business, but also a social event. There were tables full of home-baked cookies, coffee, and cider. Lots of kids and dogs.

I was taking a break, looking over the scene, and my eyes stopped on a kid who couldn't have been more than 3 years old, bundled up to the chin, standing next to a mud puddle, holding a stick. As I watched, the kid raised the stick tentatively and struck the surface of the puddle.

Made a nice splash, but not very big.

So the kid took another lick. A little harder. Much better splash. Got a little mud on his new, purple, down-filled parka.

Another lick. Much harder and much more satisfactory splash. Mud everywhere.

Now the kid had the rhythm and started beating that mud puddle like a rented mule. Mud was flying everywhere. Hell of a show. I didn't know who the kid was, but I was sure of one thing: The kid had to be a boy.

Sex Stereotyping

I admit it, I was guilty of sexual stereotyping. I was also right. "Trevor," said the kid's mother when she spotted him, "can't you please just be still, like your sister?"

Well, no, he couldn't. And anyone who has spent time around kids knows this. But we aren't allowed to know this anymore. These days, boys and girls are supposed to be the same, and you're not permitted to treat them differently.

This, anyway, is the party line of the PC loudmouths, which, increasingly, the larger culture has pliantly picked up. In the wake of the recent triumph of the U.S. women's team in World Cup soccer, a major corporation tried to cash in on this sentiment with a refrigerator commercial showing a couple viewing their unborn child via a sonogram. When he learns that he will soon be Dad to a little girl, the man's attitude is, "Makes no difference; we'll play sports together just the same as if she were my son."

My thought when I watched this commercial was that although this guy may love his new fridge, he'll end up one disappointed father. Either that or he'll learn the facts of life pretty quickly. Starting with. . . .

Realistic Expectations

Don't let your expectations get the best of you. I base this on nothing more scientific than my own experience. For no good reason, I was expecting boys. I got girls. Two of them. I had visions of hunting and fishing, playing catch, and camping with my boys. I had profoundly happy memories of doing those things with my own father, and I wanted to re-live the experience with my sons. In the bewildering, slightly giddy days of my early fatherhood, I listened to prevailing wisdom, telling myself I was lucky to live in an age when stereotypes didn't matter.

One of the things we did, as soon as possible, was buy our children toys that were meant to reinforce the idea that the kids didn't know whether they were boys or girls and would thus make their own choices. In the laboratory of our play-room, however, we learned pretty quickly that boys would play with trucks and girls would play with dolls. I've watched a young nephew of mine, the child of thoroughly modern parents, sit enthralled in front of a construction video that shows lots of D-9s, front-end loaders, and backhoes. His sis-ter would rather take a nap than watch that video.

Fight biology and you get zapped. There were some hold-outs, grim ideologues who would try to interest girls in fire engines instead of Barbie. One boy—whose mother did not allow toy guns in her home—routinely found sticks shaped like pistols and shot the hell out of his playmates when he was at our house. Shot his mom, too, when she came to pick him up.

So I quit buying trucks and such for my girls and started coming home from business trips with presents that worked in their dollhouse. I got a lot more mileage out of a minia-ture four-poster than out of a cap gun.

A Girl Thing

Girls like that their dads are different from them (as much as boys like that they're not). I learned that taking things apart and (sometimes) putting them back together wasn't generally a girl thing. When boys came over to play, they'd leave a trail of disassembled toys behind, something my girls almost never did.

"He was a good boy," as someone once famously said. "I just couldn't think of enough things to tell him not to do."

Men Are Dominant, Women Are Submissive

Temperamentally, men are inclined toward dominance, rank-related aggression (competitiveness), independence, psychopathy and sensation-seeking. Women are inclined toward submission, defensive aggression, attachment and nurturance, anxiety and security-seeking.

Charley Reese, *Conservative Chronicle*, September 13, 1995.

But they're all a kick. Not that I quit on my girls as companions—not for a second. I took them fishing, canoeing, and even hunting. But they approached these things differently from the boys who were sometimes along. The girls liked fishing, but they would lose interest when there wasn't a lot of action. The boys—one of whom reminded me of myself at age 10—didn't care if the fish weren't biting. They'd stay at it, grimly, until I told them we had to quit. But my girls loved to clean the fish we did catch. They were never squeamish.

I taught my girls how to shoot with a BB gun, and they are both good marksmen. Still, they never became real hunters. One boy I took out hunting just wanted to shoot something and wondered what would happen if we bagged our limit. Would we find something else to hunt, or would we have to quit? My girls cared more about our dog. They loved to watch her work.

Reason and Persuasion

Boys respond to intimidation—now and then. Girls respond to reason and persuasion. When my girls were old enough, I taught them how to throw a ball and volunteered to coach their softball team. I expected coaching to amount to channeling a lot of natural exuberance and enthusiasm and then teaching technique. I was surprised, over and over, to arrive at practice and find the girls standing around talking. They had gloves and balls, but they were waiting for me to show up to tell them to start playing catch. And once I got them throwing and catching to warm up, they would lose interest after 15 or 20 minutes. I learned to break the practices up into segments, and I kept them short. I wasn't being guided by some theory, merely doing what seemed to work.

But man, were those girls coachable. You could show one of them how to take a good stance in the batter's box, and she would do it. Show her how not to "throw like a girl," and pretty soon she would be smoking it in so hard your glove popped.

When I was that age, I took coaching about as well as a rock.

Sports are what fathers and sons share instead of "intimacy." Nothing wrong with that. This different approach to sports can be crucial, since sports are often an incredible bonding agent. This works between teammates, of course, but also between fathers and sons. Fathers and sons hunted together when we were a rural, small-town culture. Now that we have become an urban and suburban society, fathers and sons play catch, shoot baskets, and follow their favorite teams together.

Men who believe that they will form exactly that bond with their daughters are usually setting themselves up for disappointment, even if their daughters go on to play World Cup soccer. The difference is fundamental, encoded within us. Men are aggressive and hierarchical, women nurturing and cooperative. That's how nature, which knew exactly what it was doing, wanted it.

Balance and Brute Force

Balance and brute force make the world go round. Does all this mean that some form of this bond is impossible? That you are stuck with the old roles, in which your daughter is your princess and you are her hero and the two of you will never be any kind of companions?

No. I learned this from experience, too. My daughters and I go scuba diving together. We still fish together. A few years ago, my older daughter and I started rock climbing together. Women make great climbers, a guide once told me, because they have better balance than men and don't tend to rely on strength. My daughter quickly surpassed me in skill. . . . We spent a month on a 23,000-foot mountain on which 16 climbers had died the year before. She made the summit before I did and was waiting for me with a hug when I got there.

It was a sublime moment. No earthly way it could have been better if she'd been my son. And she knew it.

Still, not once over the years have I experienced an altogether different kind of pleasure: that of seeing my own child trying to beat a puddle into submission with a stick.

*"The evolutionary and ethnographic world
offers a fascinating diversity of cultural
constructions of gender."*

Culture Establishes Gender Roles

Michael S. Kimmel

In the following viewpoint Michael S. Kimmel argues that
cultural mores determine male and female roles. Various cultures in Africa and Asia, he contends, produce gender roles
that differ from those in Western societies, evidence that
gender roles are culturally determined. For example, he cites
one culture, the Tchambuli, studied by anthropologist Margaret Mead, in which women are the economic providers and
men spend their days primping and shopping. He concludes
that gender roles are determined more by one's environment
than by one's sex. Kimmel is the author of *The Gendered Society*, from which this viewpoint was excerpted.

As you read, consider the following questions:
1. As stated by the author, how did the Mundugamor differ
   from the Arapesh?
2. What is female circumcision, as defined by Kimmel?
3. How does the author define purdah?

Michael S. Kimmel, *The Gendered Society*. New York: Oxford University Press,
2000. Copyright © 2000 by Michael S. Kimmel. Reproduced by permission of
the publisher.

Biological models assume that sex determines gender, that innate biological differences lead to behavioral differences which lead to social arrangements. By this account, social inequalities are encoded into our physiological composition. Biological anomalies alone should account for variation. But the evidence suggests otherwise. When children like the Dominican pseudohermaphrodites are raised as the other *gender* they can easily make the transition to the other *sex*. And how do we account for the dramatic differences in the definitions of masculinity and femininity around the world? And how come some societies have much wider levels of gender inequality than others? On these questions, the biological record is mute.

What's more, biology is not without its own biases, though these are often hard to detect. Some anthropologists argue that biological models projected contemporary western values onto other cultures. These projections led evolutionists like Steven Goldberg to ignore the role of women and the role of colonialism in establishing gender differences in traditional cultures. Anthropologists like Karen Sacks suggest that biological researchers always assumed that gender *difference* implied gender *inequality*, since western notions of difference do usually lead to and justify inequality. In other words, gender difference is the *result* of gender inequality—not the other way around.

Anthropological research on cultural variations in the development of gender definitions arose, in part, in response to such casual biological determinism. The more we found out about other cultures, the more certain patterns emerged. The evolutionary and ethnographic world offers a fascinating diversity of cultural constructions of gender. Yet, some themes do remain constant. Virtually all societies manifest some amount of difference between women and men, and virtually all exhibit some form of male domination, despite variations in gender definition. So, anthropologists have also tried to explore the link between the near-universals of gender difference and gender inequality. Some search for those few societies in which women hold positions of power; others examined those rituals, beliefs, customs, and practices that tend to increase inequality and those that tend to decrease it.

The Variations in Gender Definitions

When anthropologists began to explore the cultural landscape, they found far more variability in the definitions of masculinity and femininity than any biologist would have predicted. Men possessed relatively similar levels of testosterone, with similar brain structure and lateralization, yet they seemed to exhibit dramatically different levels of aggression, violence, and, especially, aggression toward women. Women, with similar brains, hormones, and ostensibly similar evolutionary imperatives, have widely varying experiences of passivity, PMS, and spatial coordination. One of the most celebrated anthropologists to explore these differences was Margaret Mead, whose research in the South Seas (Samoa, Polynesia, Indonesia) remains, despite some significant criticism, an example of engaged scholarship, clear writing, and important ideas. Mead was clear that sex differences were "not something deeply biological," but rather were learned, and once learned, became part of the ideology that continued to perpetuate them. Here's how she put it:

> I have suggested that certain human traits have been socially specialized as the appropriate attitudes and behavior of only one sex, while other human traits have been specialized for the opposite sex. This social specialization is then rationalized into a theory that the socially decreed behavior is natural for one sex and unnatural for the other, and that the deviant is a deviant because of glandular defect, or developmental accident.

In *Sex and Temperament in Three Primitive Societies* (1935), Mead explored the differences in those definitions, while in several other books, such as *Male and Female* (1949) and *Coming of Age in Samoa* (1928), she explored the processes by which males and females become the men and women their cultures prescribe. No matter what she seemed to be writing about, though, Mead always had one eye trained on the United States. In generating implicit comparisons between our own and other cultures, Mead defied us to maintain the fiction that what we observe in the United States is "natural" and cannot be changed.

In *Sex and Temperament*, Mead directly took on the claims of biological inevitability. By examining three very different cultures in New Guinea, she hoped to show the enormous cultural variation possible in definitions of masculinity and femininity, and, in so doing, enable Americans to better understand both the cultural origins and the malleability of their own ideas. The first two cultures exhibited remarkable similarities between women and men. Masculinity and femininity were not the lines along which personality differences seemed to be organized. Women and men were not "opposite" sexes. For example, all members of the Arapesh culture appeared gentle, passive, and emotionally warm. Males and females were equally "happy, trustful, confident," [according to Mead] and individualism was relatively absent. Men and women shared child rearing; both were "maternal," and both discouraged aggressiveness among boys and girls. Both men and women were thought to be relatively equally sexual, though their sexual relationships tended to be "domestic" and not "romantic" nor, apparently, what we might call passionate. Although infanticide of female babies and male polygamy were not unknown, marriage was "even and contented." Indeed, Mead pronounced the political arrangements "utopian." Here's how she summed up Arapesh life:

> quiet and uneventful co-operation, singing in the cold dawn, and singing and laughter in the evening, men who sit happily playing to themselves on hand-drums, women holding suckling children to their breasts, young girls walking easily down the centre of the village, with the walk of those who are cherished by all about them.

The Mundugamor

By contrast, Mead details how the Mundugamor, a tribe of headhunters and cannibals, also viewed women and men as similar, but expected both sexes to be equally aggressive and violent. Women showed little "maternal instinct"; they detested pregnancy and nursing, and could hardly wait to return to the serious business of work and war. "Mundugamor women actively dislike child-bearing, and they dislike children," Mead writes. "Children are carried in harsh opaque baskets that scratch their skins, later, high on their mother's shoulders, well away from the breast." Among the Mundugamor, there was a violent rivalry between fathers and sons (there was more infanticide of boys than of girls), and everyone experienced a fear that they were being wronged by others. Quite wealthy (partly as a result of their methods of population control), the Mundugamor were, as Mead concludes, "violent, competitive, aggressively sexual, jealous, ready to see and avenge insult, delighting in display, in action, in fighting."

Gender Blueprints

Regardless of their possession of X or Y chromosomes, we base judgments of gender on people's appearance—their secondary sex characteristics, their demeanor, their style of dress, their hair. We all hold in our minds a blueprint of our perceptions of femininity and masculinity. In a nutshell, femininity consists of having longish hair; wearing makeup, skirts, jewelry and high heels; walking with a wiggle; having little or no observable body hair; and being in general soft, rounded (but not too rounded) and sweet smelling.

Jennifer Reid Maxcy Myhre, *Listen Up: Voices from the Next Feminist Generation*, ed. Barbara Findlen. Seattle: Seal Press, 1995.

Here, then, were two tribes that saw gender differences as virtually nonexistent—though the two cultures could hardly have been more different. The third culture Mead described was the Tchambuli, where, as in the United States, women and men were seen as extremely different. This was a patrilineal culture in which polygyny was accepted. Here, one sex was composed primarily of nurturing and gossipy consumers who spent their days dressing up and going shopping. They wore curls and lots of jewelry, and Mead describes them as "charming, graceful, coquettish." These, incidentally, were the men, and they liked nothing better than to "go off resplendent in feathers and shell ornaments to spend a delightful few days" shopping. The women were dominant and energetic, the economic providers. It was they who fished, an activity upon which the entire culture depended, and it was they "who have the real positions of power in the society." Completely unadorned, they were efficient, businesslike, controlled all the commerce and diplomacy of the culture, and were the initiators of sexual relations. Mead notes that the Tchambuli were the only culture she had ever seen "where little girls of ten and eleven were more alertly intelligent and more enterprising than little boys." She writes that "[w]hat the women will think, what the women will say, what the women will do lies at the back of each man's mind as he weaves his tenuous and uncertain web of insubstantial relations with other men." By contrast, "the women are a solid group, confused by no rivalries, brisk, patronizing, and jovial."

What Mead found, then, were two cultures in which women and men were seen as similar, and one culture in which they were seen as extremely different from each other, but the reverse of the model familiar to us. Each culture, of course, believed that women and men were the way they were because their biological sex *determined* their personality. None of them believed that they were the outcome of economic scarcity, military success, or cultural arrangements. . . .

Rituals of Gender

One of the ways that anthropologists have explored the cultural construction of gender is by examining specific gender rituals. Their work suggests that the origins of these rituals lie in nonbiological places. Since questions of reproduction and child rearing loom so large in the determination of gender inequality, it makes sense that a lot of these rituals are concerned with reproduction. And since spatial segregation seems to be highly associated with gender difference and gender inequality, ritual segregation—either in space or in time—may have also been a focus of attention. For example, the initiation of young males has been of particular concern, in part because of the relative disappearance of such formal cultural rituals in the contemporary United States. Initiation rituals provide a sense of identity and group membership to the men who participate in them. Many cultures, especially settled agricultural and pastoral societies, include circumcision, the excision of the foreskin of a boy's penis, in a ritual incorporating a male into the society. The age of this ceremony varies; one survey of twenty-one cultures that practice circumcision found that four perform it in infancy, ten when the boy is about ten years old (before puberty), six perform it at puberty, and one waits until late adolescence.

Why would so many cultures determine that membership in the world of adult men requires genital mutilation? Indeed, circumcision is the most common medical procedure in the United States. Theories, of course, abound. In the Jewish Bible, circumcision is a visible sign of the bond between God and man, a symbol of man's obedience to God's law. (In Gen. 17:10–11, 14, God commands Abraham to circumcise Isaac as a covenant.) But it also seems to have been seen as a trophy. Successful warriors would cut off their foes' foreskins to symbolize their victory, and to permanently disfigure and humiliate the vanquished foe. (In 1 Sam. 18:25, King Saul demands that David slay one hundred enemies and bring back their foreskins as a bride-price. David, a bit overeager, brings back two hundred.)

In other cultures, ethnographers suggest that circumcision creates a visible scar that binds men to one another, and serves as a rite of passage to adult masculinity. [Anthropologists John W.] Whiting, [Richard] Kluckhohn, and [Albert] Anthony argue that it symbolically serves to sever a boy's emotional ties to his mother, and therefore to assure appropriate masculine identification. Other writers point out that cultures that emphasize circumcision of young males tend to be those where both gender differentiation and gender inequality are greatest. Circumcision, which is always a public ceremony, simultaneously cements the bonds between father (and his generation) and son (and his generation), links the males together, and excludes women, visibly and demonstrably. Circumcision, then, tends to be associated with male domination, as do other forms of male genital mutilation. In a very few cultures, for example, the penis is ritually bled by cutting. Such cultures still believe in bleeding as a cure for illness—in this case, illness brought about by sexual contact with women, who are believed to be impure and infectious. And we know of four cultures that practice hemicastration, the removal of one testicle. In one culture, people believe it prevents the birth of twins.

Female Circumcision

Female "circumcision" is also practiced in several cultures, though far fewer than male circumcision. This consists either of clitoridectomy, in which the clitoris is cut away, or infibulation, in which the labia majora are sewn together with only a very small opening left to allow for urination. It is interesting that female circumcision is often performed by adult women. In other cultures, it is performed by the brother of the girl's father. Clitoridectomy is widespread in Africa, but few other places, and it invariably takes place in societies that also practice male circumcision. Infibulation seems to be most widely practiced in East Africa and Somalia, and its goal is to prevent sexual intercourse, while the goal of clitoridectomy is simply to prevent sexual pleasure, and thereby sexual promiscuity. Here is the description of the practice from one who underwent it, a Sudanese woman now working as a teacher in the Middle East:

I will never forget the day of my circumcision, which took place forty years ago. I was six years old. One morning during my school summer vacation, my mother told me that I had to go with her to her sisters' house and then to visit a sick relative in Halfayat El Mulook [in the northern part of Khartoum, Sudan]. We did go to my aunts' house, and from there all of us went straight to [a] red brick house [I had never seen].

While my mother was knocking, I tried to pronounce the name that was on the door. Soon enough I realized that it was Haija Alamin's house. She was the midwife who [performed circumcisions] on girls in my neighborhood. I was petrified and tried to break loose. But I was captured and subdued by my mother and two aunts. They began to tell me that the midwife was going to purify me.

The midwife was the cruelest person I had seen . . . [She] ordered her young maid to go buy razors from the Yemeni grocer next door. I still remember her when she came back with the razors, which were enveloped in purple wrappings with a crocodile drawing on it.

The women ordered me to lie down on a bed [made of ropes] that had a little hole in the middle. They held me tight while the midwife started to cut my flesh without anesthetics. I screamed till I lost my voice. The midwife was saying to me "Do you want me to be taken into police custody?" After the job was done I could not eat, drink, or even pass urine for three days. I remember one of my uncles who discovered what they did to me threatened to press charges against his sisters. They were afraid of him and they decided to bring me back to the midwife. In her sternest voice she ordered me to squat on the floor and urinate. It seemed like the most difficult thing to do at that point, but I did it. I urinated for a long time and was shivering with pain.

34

It took a very long time [before] I was back to normal. I understand the motives of my mother, that she wanted me to be clean, but I suffered a lot.

The Purpose of Circumcision Rituals

It is interesting that both cultures that circumcise men and those that circumcise women tend to be those where men's status is highest. The purpose of the ritual reveals some of this difference. For men, it is a marking that simultaneously shows that all men are biologically *and culturally* alike—and that they are different from women. Thus it can be seen as reinforcing male dominance. Historically, there was some evidence that male circumcision was medically beneficial, as it reduced the possibilities of penile infection by removing the foreskin, a place where bacteria could congregate. This is no longer the case; rates of penile infection or urethral cancer show little difference between those who have or have not been circumcised. Among advanced industrial societies, only in the United States are the majority of men circumcised, although that rate has dropped from over 95 percent in the 1960s to about two-thirds today. Australia has the second highest rate, about 10 percent.

For women, circumcision has never been justified by medical benefits; it directly impedes adequate sexual functioning and is designed to curtail sexual pleasure. Female circumcision is nearly always performed when women reach puberty, that is, when they are capable of experiencing sexual pleasure, and seems to be associated with men's control over women's sexuality. Currently, political campaigns are being waged to prohibit female genital mutilation as a violation of women's human rights. However, many of its defenders suggest that such campaigns are motivated by Western values. They insist that afterwards, women are revered and respected as members of the culture. (There are no widespread political campaigns against male circumcision, though some individuals have recently begun to rethink the ritual as a form of genital mutilation, and a few men are even undergoing a surgical procedure designed to replace the lost foreskin.)

One of the more interesting theories about the prevalence of these reproductive and sexual rituals has been offered by

Jeffrey and Karen Paige in their book *The Politics of Reproductive Ritual.* Paige and Paige offer a materialist interpretation of these rituals, locating the origins of male circumcision, couvade, and purdah in the culture's relationship with its immediate material environment. Take couvade, for example. This is a ritual that men observe when their wives are having babies. Generally, they observe the same food taboos as their wives, restrict their ordinary activities, and even seclude themselves during their wives' delivery and postpartum period. What could possibly be the point of this? Some might think it is anthropologically "cute," as the men often even imitate the symptoms of pregnancy, in apparent sympathy for their wives. But Paige and Paige see it differently. They argue that couvade is significant in cultures where there are no legal mechanisms to keep the couple together or to assure paternity. Couvade is a way for men to fully claim paternity, to know that the baby is theirs. It is also a vehicle by which the men can control women's sexuality by appropriating control over paternity.

Paige and Paige also examine the politics of purdah, the Islamic requirement that women conceal themselves at all times. Ostensibly, this is to protect women's chastity and men's honor—women must be completely covered because they "are so sexy, so tempting, so incapable of controlling their emotions and sexuality, the men say, that they are a danger to the social order." It is as if by concealing women, they can harness women's sexuality. But this is only half the story. It also suggests that *men* are so susceptible to temptation, so incapable of resistance, such easy prey, that they are likely to fall into temptation at any time. In order to protect women from *men's* sexual rapaciousness, men must control women and take away the source of the temptation. . . .

If the anthropologists have demonstrated anything, it is the rich diversity in human cultural arrangements and the disparate definitions of gender and sexuality that we have produced within our cultures. Several theories explain the historical origins of these patterns and suggest ways we can modify or abandon some historically coercive or exploitative practices without doing damage to our evolutionary legacy. Cultural relativism also suggests that, in this enormous cultural variety and historical evolution of custom and culture, we shed those customs we no longer need, even if once they served some societal purpose. "Assertions of past inferiority for women should therefore be irrelevant to present and future developments," writes [anthropologist] Eleanor Leacock.

"I imagine a future in which . . . genders have multiplied beyond currently fathomable limits."

The Idea of Multiple Genders Must Be Accepted

Anne Fausto-Sterling

According to Anne Fausto-Sterling in the following viewpoint, gender variations do not always fit into male and female categories. Despite society's insistence on dichotomous gender rules, she maintains, many people such as homosexuals and intersexuals do not fit into those categories and suffer because of it. For example she contends that intersexuals, individuals who have both male and female sexual characteristics, are stigmatized because their sex organs cannot be labeled strictly male or female. Fausto-Sterling claims that as American society becomes more secular, the laws regulating marriage and sexual relations—which reinforce dichotomous gender rules—will eventually accommodate instead a range of genders. Fausto-Sterling is the author of *Sexing the Body: Gender Politics and the Construction of Sexuality*, from which this viewpoint was excerpted.

As you read, consider the following questions:
1. What sexual categories, in addition to male and female, does Fausto-Sterling propose?
2. How does the author define transgenderism?
3. What legal protections does the author suggest to ease the transition to a gender-diverse society?

Anne Fausto-Sterling, *Sexing the Body: Gender Politics and the Construction of Sexuality*. New York: Basic Books, 2000. Copyright © 2000 by Basic Books, a member of the Perseus Books Group. All rights reserved. Reproduced by permission.

In 1993 I published a modest proposal suggesting that we replace our two-sex system with a five-sex one. In addition to males and females, I argued, we should also accept the categories herms (named after "true" hermaphrodites), merms (named after male "pseudo-hermaphrodites"), and ferms (named after female "pseudo-hermaphrodites"). I'd intended to be provocative, but I had also been writing tongue in cheek, and so was surprised by the extent of the controversy the article unleashed. Right-wing Christians somehow connected my idea of five sexes to the United Nations–sponsored 4th World Conference on Women, to be held in Beijing two years later, apparently seeing some sort of global conspiracy at work. "It is maddening," says the text of a *New York Times* advertisement paid for by the Catholic League for Religious and Civil Rights, "to listen to discussions of 'five genders' when every sane person knows there are but two sexes, both of which are rooted in nature."

[Sexologist] John Money was also horrified by my article, although for different reasons. In a new edition of his guide for those who counsel intersexual children and their families, he wrote: "In the 1970's nurturists . . . became . . . 'social constructionists.' They align themselves against biology and medicine. . . . They consider all sex differences as artifacts of social construction. In cases of birth defects of the sex organs, they attack all medical and surgical interventions as unjustified meddling designed to force babies into fixed social molds of male and female. . . . One writer has gone even to the extreme of proposing that there are five sexes . . . (Fausto-Sterling)." Meanwhile, those battling against the constraints of our sex/gender system were delighted by the article. The science fiction writer Melissa Scott wrote a novel entitled *Shadow Man*, which includes nine types of sexual preference and several genders, including fems (people with testes, XY chromosomes, and some aspects of female genitalia), herms (people with ovaries and testes), and mems (people with XX chromosomes and some aspects of male genitalia). Others used the idea of five sexes as a starting point for their own multi-gendered theories.

Clearly I had struck a nerve. The fact that so many people could get riled up by my proposal to revamp our sex/gender system suggested change (and resistance to it) might be in the offing. Indeed, a lot *has* changed since 1993, and I like to think that my article was one important stimulus. Intersexuals have materialized before our very eyes, like beings beamed up onto the Starship Enterprise. They have become political organizers lobbying physicians and politicians to change treatment practices. More generally, the debate over our cultural conceptions of gender has escalated, and the boundaries separating masculine and feminine seem harder than ever to define. Some find the changes under way deeply disturbing; others find them liberating. . . .

A Weak Case

Those who defend current approaches to the management of intersexuality can, at best, offer a weak case for continuing the status quo.[1] Many patients are scarred—both psychologically and physically—by a process heavy on surgical prowess and light on explanation, psychological support, and full disclosure. We stand now at a fork in the road. To the right we can walk toward reaffirmation of the naturalness of the number 2 and continue to develop new medical technology, including gene "therapy" and new prenatal interventions to ensure the birth of only two sexes. To the left, we can hike up the hill of natural and cultural variability. Traditionally, in European and American culture we have defined two genders, each with a range of permissible behaviors; but things have begun to change. There are househusbands and women fighter pilots. There are feminine lesbians and gay men both buff and butch. Male to female and female to male transsexuals render the sex/gender divide virtually unintelligible.

The Five Sexes

All of which brings me back to the five sexes. I imagine a future in which our knowledge of the body has led to resistance against medical surveillance, in which medical science

1. Intersexuality is defined as having sexual characteristics intermediate between those of a typical male and a typical female. Doctors currently manage cases of intersexuality by surgically assigning a gender to a newborn intersexual. These procedures are controversial because they can cause scarring and lifelong pain. In addition, many intersexuals contend that they were assigned the wrong sex and grew up feeling trapped in the wrong body.

has been placed at the service of gender variability, and genders have multiplied beyond currently fathomable limits. [Psychology professor] Suzanne Kessler suggests that "gender variability can . . . be seen . . . in a new way—as an expansion of what is meant by male and female." Ultimately, perhaps, concepts of masculinity and femininity might overlap so completely as to render the very notion of gender difference irrelevant.

Sex Versus Gender

Often, the words "sex" and "gender" are mistakenly used synonymously in our society. This usage, however, is erroneous. Sex refers to the biological characteristics of a person, whereas gender refers to what society imposes onto a person based on their sex.

Alex Gino, *Daily Pennsylvanian*, September 24, 1998.

In the future, the hierarchical divisions between patient and doctor, parent and child, male and female, heterosexual and homosexual will dissolve. The critical voices of [intersexed] people . . . all point to cracks in the monolith of current medical writings and practice. It is possible to envision a new ethic of medical treatment, one that permits ambiguity to thrive, rooted in a culture that has moved beyond gender hierarchies. In my utopia, an intersexual's major medical concerns would be the potentially life-threatening conditions that sometimes accompany intersex development, such as salt imbalance due to adrenal malfunction, higher frequencies of gonadal tumors, and hernias. Medical intervention aimed at synchronizing body image and gender identity would only rarely occur before the age of reason. Such technological intervention would be a cooperative venture among physician, patient, and gender advisers. As Kessler has noted, the unusual genitalia of intersexuals could be considered to be "intact" rather than "deformed"; surgery, seen now as a creative gesture (surgeons "create" a vagina), might be seen as destructive (tissue is destroyed and removed) and thus necessary only when life is at stake.

Accepted treatment approaches damage both mind and body. And clearly, it is possible for healthy adults to emerge from a childhood in which genital anatomy does not completely match sex of rearing. But still, the good doctors are skeptical. So too are many parents and potential parents. It is impossible not to personalize the argument. What if you had an intersexual child? Could you and your child become pioneers in a new management strategy? Where, in addition to the new intersexual rights activists, might you look for advice and inspiration?

The History of Transsexualism

The history of transsexualism offers food for thought. In European and American culture we understand transsexuals to be individuals who have been born with "good" male or "good" female bodies. Psychologically, however, they envision themselves as members of the "opposite" sex. A transsexual's drive to have his/her body conform with his/her psyche is so strong that many seek medical aid to transform their bodies hormonally and ultimately surgically, by removal of their gonads and transformation of their external genitalia. The demands of self-identified transsexuals have contributed to changing medical practices, forcing recognition and naming of the phenomenon. Just as the idea that homosexuality is an inborn, stable trait did not emerge until the end of the nineteenth century, the transsexual did not fully emerge as a special type of person until the middle of the twentieth. Winning the right to surgical and legal sex changes, however, exacted a price: the reinforcement of a two-gender system. By requesting surgery to make their bodies match their gender, transsexuals enacted the logical extreme of the medical profession's philosophy that within an individual's body, sex, and gender must conform. Indeed, transsexuals had little choice but to view themselves within this framework if they wanted to obtain surgical help. To avoid creating a "lesbian" marriage, physicians in gender clinics demanded that married transsexuals divorce before their surgery. Afterwards, they could legally change their birth certificates to reflect their new status.

Within the past ten to twenty years, however, the edifice of transsexual dualism has developed large cracks. Some transsexual organizations have begun to support the concept of *transgenderism*, which constitutes a more radical re-visioning of sex and gender. Whereas traditional transsexuals might describe a male transvestite—a man dressing in women's clothing—as a transsexual on the road to becoming a complete female, transgenderists accept "kinship among those with gender-variant identities. Transgenderism supplants the dichotomy of transsexual and transvestite with a concept of continuity," [according to sexologist Alfred Kinsey]. Earlier generations of transsexuals did not want to depart from gender norms, but rather to blend totally into their new gender role. Today, however, many argue that they need to come out as transsexuals, permanently assuming a transsexual identity that is neither male nor female in the traditional sense.

Within the transgender community (which has its own political organizations and even its own electronic bulletin board on the Internet), gender variations abound. Some choose to become women while keeping their male genitals intact. Many who have undergone surgical transformation have taken up homosexual roles. For example, a male-to-female transsexual may come out as a lesbian (or a female-to-male as a gay male). Consider Jane, born a physiological male, now in her late thirties, living with her wife (whom she married when her name was still John). Jane takes hormones to feminize herself, but they have not yet interfered with her ability to have erections and intercourse as a man. [According to political scientist Mary Hawkesworth:]

> From her perspective, Jane has a lesbian relationship with her wife (Mary). Yet she also uses her penis for pleasure. Mary does not identify herself as a lesbian, although she maintains love and attraction for Jane, whom she regards as the same person she fell in love with although this person has changed physically. Mary regards herself as heterosexual . . . although she defines sexual intimacy with her spouse Jane as somewhere between lesbian and heterosexual. . . .

The Problem with Gender

Is it so unreasonable to ask that we focus more clearly on variability and pay less attention to gender conformity? The problem with gender, as we now have it, is the violence—both real and metaphorical—we do by generalizing. No woman or man fits the universal gender stereotype. "It might be more useful," writes the sociologist Judith Lorber, ". . . to group patterns of behavior and only then look for identifying markers of the people likely to enact such behaviors."

Were we in Europe and America to move to a multiple sex and gender role system (as it seems we might be doing), we would not be cultural pioneers. Several Native American cultures, for example, define a third gender, which may include people whom we would label as homosexual, transsexual, or intersexual but also people we would label as male or female. Anthropologists have described other groups, such as the Hijras of India, that contain individuals whom we in the West would label intersexes, transsexuals, effeminate men, and eunuchs. As with the varied Native American categories, the Hijras vary in their origins and gender characteristics. Anthropologists debate about how to interpret Native American gender systems. What is important, however, is that the existence of other systems suggests that ours is not inevitable. . . .

Toward the End of Gender Tyranny

Simply recognizing a third category does not assure a flexible gender system. Such flexibility requires political and social struggle. In discussing my "five sexes" proposal Suzanne Kessler drives home this point with great effect:

> The limitation with Fausto-Sterling's proposal is that legitimizing other sets of genitals . . . still gives genitals primary signifying status and ignores the fact that in the everyday world gender attributions are made without access to genital inspection . . . what has primacy in everyday life is the gender that is performed, regardless of the flesh's configuration under the clothes.

Kessler argues that it would be better for intersexuals and their supporters to turn everyone's focus away from genitals and to dispense with claims to a separate intersexual identity. Instead, she suggests, men and women would come in a wider assortment. Some women would have large clitorises or fused labia, while some men would have "small penises or misshapen scrota—phenotypes with no particular clinical or identity meaning, [Kessler suggests]." I think Kessler is right, and this is why I am no longer advocating using discrete categories such as herm, merm, and ferm, even tongue in cheek.

The intersexual or transgender person who presents a social gender—what Kessler calls "cultural genitals"—that conflicts with his/her physical genitals often risks his/her life. In a recent court case, a mother charged that her son, a transvestite, died because paramedics stopped treating him after discovering his male genitals. The jury awarded her $2.9 million in damages. While it is heartening that a jury found such behavior unacceptable, the case underscores the high risk of gender transgression. "Transgender warriors," as [transgender activist] Leslie Feinberg calls them, will continue to be in danger until we succeed in moving them onto the "acceptable" side of the imaginary line separating "normal, natural, holy" gender from the "abnormal, unnatural, sick [and] sinful."

Thinking Outside the Gender Box

A person with ovaries, breasts, and a vagina, but whose "cultural genitals" are male also faces difficulties. In applying for a license or passport, for instance, one must indicate "M" or "F" in the gender box. Suppose such a person checks "F" on his or her license and then later uses the license for identification. The 1998 murder in Wyoming of homosexual Matthew Shepherd makes clear the possible dangers. A masculine-presenting female is in danger of violent attack if she does not "pass" as male. Similarly, she can get into legal trouble if stopped for a traffic violation or passport control, as the legal authority can accuse her of deception—masquerading as a male for possibly illegal purposes. In the 1950s, when police raided lesbian bars, they demanded that women be wearing three items of women's clothing in order to avoid arrest. As Feinberg notes, we have not moved very far beyond that moment.

Given the discrimination and violence faced by those whose cultural and physical genitals don't match, legal protections are needed during the transition to a gender-diverse utopia. It would help to eliminate the "gender" category from licenses, passports, and the like. The transgender activist Leslie Feinberg writes: "Sex categories should be removed from all basic identification papers—from driver's licenses to passports—and since the right of each person to define their own sex is so basic, it should be eliminated from birth certificates as well." Indeed, why are physical genitals necessary for identification? Surely attributes both more visible (such as height, build, and eye color) and less visible (fingerprints and DNA profiles) would be of greater use.

Transgender activists have written "An International Bill of Gender Rights" that includes (among ten gender rights) "the right to define gender identity, the right to control and change one's own body, the right to sexual expression and the right to form committed, loving relationships and enter into marital contracts." The legal bases for such rights are being hammered out in the courts as I write, through the establishment of case law regarding sex discrimination and homosexual rights. . . .

The Homosexual Connection

As usual, the debates over intersexuality are inextricable from those over homosexuality; we cannot consider the challenges one poses to our gender system without considering the parallel challenge posed by the other. In considering the potential marriage of an intersexual, the legal and medical rules often focus on the question of homosexual marriage. In the case of *Corbett v. Corbett 1970*, April Ashley, a British transsexual, married one Mr. Corbett, who later asked the court to annul the marriage because April was really a man. April argued that she was a social female and thus eligible for marriage. The judge, however, ruled that the operation was pure artifact, imposed on a clearly male body. Not only had April Ashley been born a male, but her transforming surgery had not created a vagina large enough to permit penile penetration. Furthermore, sexual intercourse was "the institution on which the family is built, and in which the capacity for natural hetero-sexual intercourse is an essential element." "Marriage," the judge continued, "is a relationship which depends upon sex and not gender."

An earlier British case had annulled a marriage between a man and a woman born without a vagina. The husband testified that he could not penetrate more than two inches into his wife's artificial vagina. Furthermore, he claimed even that channel was artificial, not the biological one due him as a true husband. The divorce commissioner agreed, citing a much earlier case in which the judge ruled, "I am of the opinion that no man ought to be reduced to this state of quasi-natural connexion."

Both British judges declared marriage without the ability for vaginal-penile sex to be illegal, one even adding the criterion that two inches did not a penetration make. In other countries—and even in the several U.S. states that ban anal and oral contact between both same-sex and opposite-sex partners and those that restrict the ban to homosexual encounters—engaging in certain types of sexual encounters can result in felony charges. Similarly, a Dutch physician discussed several cases of XX intersexuals, raised as males, who married females. Defining them as biological females (based on their two X chromosomes and ovaries), the physician called for a discussion of the legality of the marriages. Should they be dissolved "notwithstanding the fact that they are happy ones?" Should they "be recognized legally and ecclesiastically?" [he asked].

Cultural Genitals and Physical Genitals

If cultural genitals counted for more than physical genitals, many of the dilemmas just described could be easily resolved. Since the mid-1960s the International Olympic Committee has demanded that all female athletes submit to a chromosome or DNA test, even though some scientists urge the elimination of sex testing. Whether we are deciding who may compete in the women's high jump or whether we should record sex on a newborn's birth certificate, the judgment derives primarily from social conventions. Legally, the interest of the state in maintaining a two-gender system focuses on questions of marriage, family structure, and sexual practices. But the time is drawing near when even these state concerns will seem arcane to us. Laws regulating consensual sexual behavior between adults had religious and moral origins. In the United States, at least, we are supposed to experience complete separation of church and state. As our legal system becomes further secularized (as I believe it will), it seems only a matter of time before the last laws regulating consensual bedroom behavior will become unconstitutional.

At that moment the final legal barriers to the emergence of a wide range of gender expression will disappear. . . .

My vision is utopian, but I believe in its possibility. All of the elements needed to make it come true already exist, at least in embryonic form. Necessary legal reforms are in reach, spurred forward by what one might call the "gender lobby": political organizations that work for women's rights, gay rights, and the rights of transgendered people. Medical practice has begun to change as a result of pressure from intersexual patients and their supporters. Public discussion about gender and homosexuality continues unabated with a general trend toward greater tolerance for gender multiplicity and ambiguity. The road will be bumpy, but the possibility of a more diverse and equitable future is ours if we choose to make it happen.

"Human sexuality is a dichotomy, not a continuum."

The Idea of Multiple Genders Is Wrong

Leonard Sax

In the following viewpoint Leonard Sax disputes biologist Anne Fausto-Sterling's suggestion that the number of sexes should be expanded from two to five. Sax argues that the number of intersexuals, individuals with male and female sexual characteristics, is fewer that Fausto-Sterling alleges. Thus, in Sax's opinion, the problem of gender confusion is less widespread than Fausto-Sterling claims it is. In addition, according to Sax, most exceptions to typical male and female characteristics are genetic abnormalities, not legitimate variations. He asserts that there are only two genders and to claim otherwise is disingenuous. Sax is a psychologist and family physician.

As you read, consider the following questions:

1. Why is Anne Fausto-Sterling's definition of intersex too broad, in the author's opinion?
2. How does Sax define Klinefelter syndrome?
3. What is nosology, as defined by the author?

Leonard Sax, "How Common Is Intersex? A Response to Anne Fausto-Sterling," *Journal of Sex Research*, vol. 39, August 2002, p. 174. Copyright © 2002 by the Society for the Scientific Study of Sexuality, Inc. Reproduced by permission.

Sometimes a child is born with genitalia which cannot be classified as female or male. A genetically female child (i.e., with XX chromosomes) may be born with external genitalia which appear to be those of a normal male. Or, a genetically male child (XY chromosomes) may be born with female-appearing external genitalia. In very rare cases, a child may be born with both female and male genitalia. Because these conditions are in some sense "in-between" the two sexes, they are collectively referred to as intersex.

How common is intersex? In her 1993 essay, biologist Anne Fausto-Sterling acknowledged that "it is extremely difficult to estimate the frequency of intersexuality." In this paper we will focus on establishing how often intersexual conditions occur, and what conditions should be considered intersexual.

The Continuum Argument

In her most recent book, *Sexing the Body: Gender Politics and the Construction of Sexuality*, Fausto-Sterling maintains that human sexuality is best understood not as a dichotomy but as a continuum. She bases this assertion on her beliefs regarding intersex conditions. A chapter subtitled "The Sexual Continuum" begins with the case of Levi Suydam, an intersexual living in the 1840s who menstruated regularly but who also had a penis and testicles. Fausto-Sterling writes:

> While male and female stand on the extreme ends of a biological continuum, there are many bodies, bodies such as Suydam's, that evidently mix together anatomical components conventionally attributed to both males and females. The implications of my argument for a sexual continuum are profound. If nature really offers us more than two sexes, then it follows that our current notions of masculinity and femininity are cultural conceits.
>
> . . . Modern surgical techniques help maintain the two-sex system. Today children who are born "either/or-neither/both"— a fairly common phenomenon—usually disappear from view because doctors "correct" them right away with surgery.

Fausto-Sterling asserts that 1.7% of human births are intersex. This figure was widely quoted in the aftermath of the book's publication. "Instead of viewing intersexuality as a genetic hiccup," wrote Courtney Weaver for the *Washington*

Post, "[Fausto-Sterling] points out that its frequency mandates a fresher look. In one study, intersexuality typically constitute 1.7% of a community." The *New England Journal of Medicine* applauded Fausto-Sterling's "careful and insightful book. . . . She [Fausto-Sterling] points out that intersexual newborns are not rare (they may account for 1.7% of births), so a review of our attitudes about these children is overdue . . ." "Most people believe that there are only two sex categories," went the review in *American Scientist*. "Yet 17 out of every 1,000 people fail to meet our assumption that everyone is either male or female. This is the approximate incidence of intersexuals: individuals with XY chromosomes and female anatomy, XX chromosomes and male anatomy, or anatomy that is half male and half female."

This reviewer assumed that Fausto-Sterling was using the term intersex in the usual way, the same way in which Fausto-Sterling herself used the term in her 1993 essay, "The Five Sexes": to refer either to individuals who have XY chromosomes with predominantly female anatomy, XX chromosomes with predominantly male anatomy, or ambiguous or mixed genitalia. This assumption is reasonable, because all the case histories presented in her book *Sexing the Body* describe individuals who meet these criteria. However, as we shall see, the 1.7% statistic is based on a much broader definition of intersex.

Fausto-Sterling herself has encouraged the belief that a significant fraction of the population is neither male nor female, but intersex. In an interview with the *New York Times*, she said that "I did some research and we found that maybe 1 to 2 percent of all births do not fall strictly within the tight definition of all-male or all-female. . . . there is greater human variation than supposed . . . [We should] lighten up about what it means to be male or female. We should definitely lighten up on those who fall in between because there are a lot of them."

Is Human Sexuality a Dichotomy or a Continuum?

Fausto-Sterling's argument that human sexuality is a continuum, not a dichotomy, rests in large measure on her claim that intersex births are a fairly common phenomenon. Specifically, Fausto-Sterling computes the incidence of intersexual births to be 1.7 per 100 live births, or 1.7%. To arrive at that figure, she defines as intersex any "individual who deviates from the Platonic ideal of physical dimorphism at the chromosomal, genital, gonadal, or hormonal levels."

This definition is too broad. Fausto-Sterling and her associates acknowledge that some of the individuals thus categorized as intersex "are undiagnosed because they present no symptoms." A definition of intersex which encompasses individuals who are phenotypically indistinguishable from normal is likely to confuse both clinicians and patients.

John Wiener, a urologist, has suggested defining intersex simply as "a discordance between phenotypic sex and chromosomal sex". While this definition would cover most true intersex patients, there are some rare conditions which are clearly intersex which are not captured by this definition. For example, some people are mosaics: Different cells in their body have different chromosomes. A 46,XY/46,XX mosaic is an individual in whom some cells have the male chromosomal complement (XY) and some cells have the female chromosomal complement (XX). If such an individual has both a penis and a vagina, then there is no mismatch between phenotypic sex and genotypic sex: Both the phenotype and the genotype are intersexual. Yet according to Wiener's definition, such an individual would not be intersex. A more comprehensive, yet still clinically useful definition of intersex would include those conditions in which (a) the phenotype is not classifiable as either male or female, or (b) chromosomal sex is inconsistent with phenotypic sex.

This definition is of course more clinically focussed than the definition employed by Fausto-Sterling. Using her definition of intersex as "any deviation from the Platonic ideal," she lists all the following conditions as intersex, and she provides the following estimates of incidence for each condition (number of births per 100 live births): (a) late-onset congenital adrenal hyperplasia (LOCAH), 1.5/100; (b) Klinefelter (XXY), 0.0922/100; (c) other non-XX, non-XY, excluding Turner and Klinefelter, 0.0639/100; (d) Turner syndrome (XO), 0.0369/100; (e) vaginal agenesis, 0.0169/100; (f) classic congenital adrenal hyperplasia, 0.00779/10; (g) complete androgen insensitivity, 0.0076/100; (h) true hermaphrodites, 0.0012/100; (i) idiopathic, 0.0009/100; and (j) partial androgen insensitivity, 0.00076/100 [these conditions are defined below]. The chief problem with this list is that the five most common conditions listed are not intersex conditions. If we examine these five conditions in more detail, we will see that there is no meaningful clinical sense in which these conditions can be considered intersex. "Deviation from the Platonic ideal" is, as we will see, not a clinically useful criterion for defining a medical condition such as intersex.

The second problem with this list is the neglect of the five most common of these conditions in Fausto-Sterling's book *Sexing the Body*. In her book, Fausto-Sterling draws her case histories exclusively from the ranks of individuals who are unambiguously intersex. However, using Fausto-Sterling's own figures, such individuals account for less than 0.02% of the general population. None of her case histories are drawn from the five most common conditions in her table, even though these five conditions constitute roughly 99% of the population she defines as intersex. Without these five conditions, intersex becomes a rare occurrence, occurring in fewer than 2 out of every 10,000 live births.

Classic Intersex Conditions

Among classic intersex conditions, the most common are congenital adrenal hyperplasia (CAH) and complete androgen insensitivity syndrome. According to Fausto-Sterling's figures, these two conditions occur with roughly the same frequency: about 0.008/100, or 8 births out of every 100,000. There is no dispute that these conditions are indeed intersex conditions. We discuss them here because some understanding of these conditions is essential in order to perceive how these conditions differ from the other syndromes which Fausto-Sterling includes in the category of intersex.

Complete Androgen Insensitivity Syndrome

These individuals are genetically male (XY), but owing to a defect in the androgen receptor, their cells do not respond to testosterone or other androgens. As a result, these individuals do not form male genitalia. Genetically male (XY) babies with this condition typically are born with a vaginal opening and clitoris indistinguishable from those seen in normal female (XX) babies. In almost all cases, the diagnosis is not suspected until puberty, when these "girls" are brought to medical attention because they have never menstruated. Investigation at that point will invariably reveal that these "girls" are in fact genetically male, that they have undescended testicles, and that neither the uterus nor the ovaries are present. These individuals are genotypically male, but phenotypically female.

Congenital Adrenal Hyperplasia

In this syndrome, a defect in an enzyme involved in the synthesis of adrenal hormones leads to a blockage in one synthetic pathway, giving rise to excessive production of androgenic hormones in a different pathway. These androgens will masculinize a female (XX) fetus in utero. At birth, the girl's genitalia may appear completely masculine, or, more commonly, the genitalia will be ambiguous—neither completely male nor completely female but somewhere in between.

Late-Onset Congenital Adrenal Hyperplasia

In late-onset congenital adrenal hyperplasia, the defect in the enzymatic pathway typically does not manifest itself until late childhood, adolescence, or later, and the degree of disruption is much less than in classic congenital adrenal hypertrophy. Reviewing the list of conditions which Fausto-Sterling considers to be intersex, we find that this one condition—late-onset congenital adrenal hyperplasia (LOCAH)—accounts for 88% of all those patients whom Fausto-Sterling classifies as intersex (1.5/1.7 = 88%).

From a clinician's perspective, however, LOCAH is not an intersex condition. The genitalia of these babies are normal at birth, and consonant with their chromosomes: XY males have normal male genitalia, and XX females have normal female genitalia. The average woman with this condition does not present until about 24 years of age. Men with LOCAH present later, if ever: Many go through life undetected or are discovered only incidentally. For example, if a daughter is discovered to have classic congenital adrenal hyperplasia, the parents often will be tested for evidence of overproduction of adrenal androgens, and one parent thereby may be discovered to have LOCAH. The most common presenting symptom of LOCAH in men is thinning of scalp hair, but even this symptom is seen in only 50% of men with LOCAH under 50 years of age.

Gender Is a Divine Creation

Scripture tells us how God created us before the Fall, and how He intended us to live: as males and females, reflecting His own image. We take our standards and identity from His revelation of our original nature.

The division of the sexes is not a "social construct." It's a divine creation.

Chuck Colson, *BreakPoint*, 1996.

Fausto-Sterling recognizes that if her definition of the intersexual as "an individual who deviates from the Platonic ideal of physical dimorphism" is to have any clinical relevance, then at least some patients with LOCAH must occasionally have problems which are intersexual in nature. Accordingly, she asserts that "when late-onset CAH occurs in childhood or adolescence and causes significant clitoral growth, it is quite possible that surgical intervention will ensue." The only reference given in support of this statement is a first-person account in the woman's magazine *Mademoiselle*. However, the article in *Mademoiselle* describes a phenotypically female but genotypically male (46,XY) individual with androgen insensitivity: in other words, a case of true intersexuality. LOCAH is never mentioned.

In a large-scale investigation of the natural history of LOCAH in women, the chief complaints of symptomatic women were one or more of the following: oligomenorrhea [infrequent or light menstruation], hirsutism [heavy growth of hair], infertility, or acne. These investigators noted that "in some cases, affected girls have shown mild clitoromegaly [an abnormally large clitoris], but not true genital ambiguity." Many women have no symptoms at all: "Probably many affected individuals are asymptomatic," notes another recent review. A recent study of 220 women with LOCAH found mild clitoromegaly in only 10%; moderate or severe clitoromegaly was not reported.

Sex Chromosome Abnormalities

Fausto-Sterling defines all sex chromosome complements other than XX or XY as intersex. Specifically, Fausto-Sterling includes Klinefelter syndrome, Turner syndrome, and all other non-XX, non-XY chromosomal variations in the intersex category.

Klinefelter syndrome. Babies born with Klinefelter syndrome (47,XXY) have normal male genitalia. Male secondary sexual characteristics develop normally in puberty, although the testicles typically are small. Erection and ejaculation are not impaired. Most men with Klinefelter syndrome are infertile, but an unknown proportion are fertile. Because Klinefelter syndrome is most often discovered in the course of infertility evaluation, fertile men with Klinefelter syndrome are likely to go completely undetected. [Sex researchers L. Abramsky and J. Chapple] have suggested that many men with Klinefelter syndrome are never diagnosed because they are phenotypically indistinguishable from normal (46,XY) men.

Turner syndrome. Among the most salient features of Turner syndrome (45,X) are infertility and short stature: Women with Turner syndrome who are not treated with growth hormone typically will be about 16 centimeters shorter than their predicted adult height based on parental heights [T.C. Sas and associates] have demonstrated that girls with Turner syndrome can achieve normal adult heights if daily doses of growth hormone are administered. Although most women with Turner syndrome cannot conceive a child, they can carry a child to term if a donated embryo or oocyte is implanted. Girls with Turner syndrome do not have ambiguous external genitalia (e.g., no clitoromegaly), nor do they typically experience confusion regarding their sexual identity. "A consistent feature documented in Turner's syndrome is the unambiguous identification with the female sex," according to a recent review in the *Lancet.*

Other chromosomal variants (non-XX and non-XY, excluding

Turner's and Klinefelter's). This category includes a variety of sex chromosome complements, such as XXX, XYY, and other less frequent arrangements. Fausto-Sterling considers all such conditions to be intersex. Men with an extra Y chromosome (47,XYY) are not distinguishable from normal (46,XY) men, although the average intelligence of men with this aneuploidy is lower than normal. Their fertility usually is not impaired. They are most commonly discovered in the course of evaluation for mild mental retardation or behavior problems. Likewise, women with an extra X chromosome ("triple X," 47,XXX) are fertile, although the mean intelligence of women with this aneuploidy is also probably below average. None of these chromosomal variants are associated with ambiguous genitalia, or with any confusion regarding sexual identity. There is therefore no clinical sense in which these individuals are intersex.

Vaginal Agenesis

Fausto-Sterling estimates that about 0.0169 births per 100 are characterized by vaginal agenesis (also known as vaginal atresia), a condition in which the distal third of the vagina fails to develop and is replaced by about 2 cm of fibrous tissue. According to the definition which I have proposed, vaginal agenesis is not an intersex condition. Girls born with this condition have an XX genotype and normal ovaries. In the majority of cases, vaginoplasty restores normal female vaginal anatomy. Women who have undergone vaginoplasty can and do go on to have successful term pregnancies. Nosologically, vaginal agenesis is to genital anatomy as cleft palate is to maxillofacial anatomy. Surgical correction for vaginal agenesis is conceptually no different from surgical correction for cleft palate.

How Common Is Intersex?

Subtracting these five categories—LOCAH, vaginal agenesis, Turner's syndrome, Klinefelter's syndrome, and other non-XX and non-XY aneuploidies—the incidence of intersex drops to 0.018%, almost 100 times lower than the estimate provided by Fausto-Sterling. This figure of 0.018% suggests that there are currently about 50,000 true intersexuals living in the United States. These individuals are of course entitled to the same expert care and consideration that all patients deserve. Nothing is gained, however, by pretending that there are 5,000,000 such individuals.

Is Intersex a Normal Variant or a Pathological Condition?

The most original feature of Fausto-Sterling's book is her reluctance to classify true intersex conditions as pathological. Regarding babies born with both a penis and a vagina, she writes: "Perhaps we will come to view such children as especially blessed or lucky. It is not so farfetched to think that some can become the most desirable of all possible mates, able to pleasure their partners in a variety of ways." Fausto-Sterling strongly affirms her belief that all possible combinations of sexual anatomy must be considered normal:

> Complete maleness and complete femaleness represent the extreme ends of a spectrum of possible body types. That these extreme ends are the most frequent has lent credence to the idea that they are not only natural (that is, produced by nature) but normal (that is, they represent both a statistical and a social ideal). Knowledge of biological variation, however, allows us to conceptualize the less frequent middle spaces as natural, although statistically unusual.

Nosological Confusion

Nosology is the science of the classification of diseases. The first principle of nosology is the distinction between the normal and the pathological. This principle poses real difficulties for Fausto-Sterling. She often uses the word *natural* synonymously with *normal* (for an example, see the previous paragraph). However, *natural* and *normal* are not synonyms. A cow may give birth to a two-headed or Siamese calf by natural processes, natural being understood as per Fausto-Sterling's definition as "produced by nature." Nevertheless, that two-headed calf unarguably manifests an abnormal condition.

Fausto-Sterling's insistence that all combinations of sexual anatomy be regarded as normal is reminiscent of [T.S.] Szasz's view of mental illness. Szasz insisted that mental illness is not a real biological phenomenon but merely an invention of society. Like Fausto-Sterling, Szasz was suspicious of the distinction between normal and pathological. Fausto-Sterling follows the example set by Szasz in her belief that classifications of normal and abnormal sexual anatomy are mere social conventions, prejudices which can and should be set aside by an enlightened intelligentsia.

This type of extreme social constructionism is confusing and is not helpful to clinicians, to their patients, or to their patients' families. Diluting the term intersex to include "any deviation from the Platonic ideal of sexual dimorphism" as Fausto-Sterling suggests, deprives the term of any clinically useful meaning.

The available data support the conclusion that human sexuality is a dichotomy, not a continuum. More than 99.98% of humans are either male or female. If the term intersex is to retain any clinical meaning, the use of this term should be restricted to those conditions in which chromosomal sex is inconsistent with phenotypic sex, or in which the phenotype is not classifiable as either male or female.

Periodical Bibliography

The following articles have been selected to supplement the diverse views presented in this chapter.

Natalie Angier	"Men, Women, Sex, and Darwin," *New York Times Magazine*, February 21, 1999.
Sarah Blustain	"The New Gender Wars," *Psychology Today*, November 2000.
James Bordwine	"I Do Not Permit . . ." *Tabletalk*, May 1999.
Mona Charen	"It May Not Be Destiny, but . . ." *Women's Quarterly*, Spring 1998.
Alice Domurat Dreger	"'Ambiguous Sex'—or Ambivalent Medicine? Ethical Issues in the Treatment of Intersexuality," *Hastings Center Report*, May/June 1998.
Barbara Ehrenreich	"The Real Truth About the Female," *Time*, March 8, 1999.
Lance Hardie	"Men Are Particles, Women Are Waves," *Quest*, March/April 1999.
John Hoffman	"Boys Will Be . . . Girls," *Today's Parent*, August 2003.
Suzanne Miller	"When Sexual Development Goes Awry," *World & I*, September 2000.
Iain Murray	"The New Science of Sex," *American Enterprise*, September 2003.
Christina Hoff Sommers	"Mother Nature Is Not a Feminist," *Free Inquiry*, Summer 2000.
Cathy Young	"Sex Differences Are Real—but Individual Differences Matter Even More," *Women's Freedom Network Newsletter*, May/June 1998.

CHAPTER 2

What Roles Should Women Embrace?

Chapter Preface

On March 23, 2003, three days into the 2003 war in Iraq, Iraqi soldiers took nineteen-year-old U.S. Army supply clerk Jessica Lynch prisoner. Suffering two broken legs and a head injury during the capture, Lynch sustained further injuries at the hands of the Iraqi military officers who interrogated her. On April 1, acting on a tip from a concerned Iraqi, U.S. Special Forces rescued Lynch. Lynch's story made headline news, with many claiming that her bravery in the face of brutality was proof that women should be allowed to serve in combat units. Others disagreed. The issue of whether women should serve in combat units highlights the difficulties society faces when women want to fill roles traditionally reserved for men.

Although women account for 14 percent of all soldiers and 20 percent of all recruits in the U.S. military, they are still not allowed to work in ground combat units, the only jobs now closed to women in land-based military forces. Of central concern to military officials is women's physical strength, their role as reproducers, and unit cohesiveness.

In regards to physical strength, most women are simply weaker than men. Women are, on average, four inches shorter than the average man and forty pounds lighter. Women also have around forty pounds less muscle and thirteen pounds more fat than do men. However, according to Rosemarie Skaine, author of *Women at War: Gender Issues of Americans in Combat*, "It is more important to have superior technical skill, intelligence, and training [in the military than physical strength]." A 1995 army study indicated that women can develop adequate strength if properly trained. However, many analysts argue that women soldiers' lack of physical strength is a problem for the military. According to Major James Wright, "Upper-body strength is an important component of virtually every Army task. There are still hundreds of manual-type tasks [such as moving wounded soldiers] which require strength." Brian Mitchell, author of *Women in the Military: Flirting with Disaster*, claims that "many modern military jobs still require more physical strength than most women possess."

Another point of contention in the debate about women

in combat units is women's role as mothers. Many claim it is shortsighted to send society's reproducers to the front lines to be killed, which could threaten the nation's ability to sustain its population. Other analysts are concerned that women in the military risk leaving their children without mothers. Columnist Kate O'Beirne claims that 64 percent of the public agrees that it is "unacceptable for the United States to send women with young children to the war zone." Other commentators argue that these fears are unfounded. For example, army captain Adam N. Wojack asserts that the concern over losing mothers and endangering the population is baseless because "the actual percentage of women in direct combat would probably be quite low."

A third concern is whether the presence of women on the front lines would undermine unit cohesiveness. Many fear that the presence of women will lead to sexual relations between male and female soldiers, and sexual harassment, both of which would destroy the trust and order necessary to retain combat effectiveness. In addition, Mitchell claims that because women are physically weaker than men, "men actually do more to make up for the limitations of their female coworkers," an unfairness that could lead to resentment and exhaust the resources of male soldiers. Captain Wojack concedes that integrating women into male combat units would be problematic at first, but he contends that "women and men can bond to form effective [military] units . . . as long as the women feel they will be treated equally." A 1997 RAND study seems to support his view. According to the study, "Gender differences alone did not appear to erode [unit] cohesion."

As the debate about women in the military makes clear, people hold strong views about women's proper sphere. The authors in the following chapter debate other roles open to women. To be sure, the capture of Jessica Lynch during the Iraq war fueled an already heated debate about women's roles in society.

"If our society is to be revitalized, the committed, religious, stay-at-home mother will have to be at the forefront."

Women Should Be Encouraged to Be Stay-at-Home Mothers

Sibyl Niemann

According to Sibyl Niemann in the following viewpoint, women should stay at home with their children if they have the financial means to do so. She contends that although full-time mothering is often lonely, frustrating, and boring, mothers have a responsibility to provide their children with the best care possible. In Niemann's opinion, a mother's care is always superior to day care. Niemann, who has four children, is a stay-at-home mother.

As you read, consider the following questions:
1. How does Niemann define a stay-at-home mother?
2. In what way is full-time mothering lonely, in the author's opinion?
3. Why does a stay-at-home mother's efforts often seem pointless, according to Niemann?

Sibyl Niemann, "The Necessary Mother," *First Things*, May 2003, p. 18. Copyright © 2003 by the Institute on Religion and Public Life. Reproduced by permission.

The baby was extra clingy today. At eighteen months, Monica has just this week cut two of her three emerging molars, which had been bulging and sore for weeks. She did not want to be put down and kept coming to grab my legs as I tried to make sandwiches for the older children, unload the dishwasher, fold laundry. Every time I nursed her, she looked intently into my face, willing me to quiet myself, unwind my attention from the rest of life, and give her the one thing in the whole world that no one else can give: my undivided, loving attention.

But today was a hard day. Last night I'd stayed up much too late reading (one of the habits of my premotherhood life that I have not been quite willing to give up), and got up several times to comfort Monica after the Tylenol wore off around 2 A.M. All morning the children quarreled, and mediating between the irrationality of three-year-old Jonah and the legalism of five-year-old Abigail had just about done me in. Of course, then there was the Trouble with the Fruit Drawer, which entailed moving the entire refrigerator just to get the door closed again. No amount of coffee helped me today.

By three this afternoon, as I drove over to pick up Abigail from kindergarten, I was neck-deep in self-pity. Why did I think that this was what I wanted? What was so bad about wearing panty hose and working for pay? Wasn't I accomplishing more? So much of my day is taken up with triviality, frustration, and minutiae!

When I got home I realized I'd forgotten to take the meat out of the freezer. Then the cat threw up. But I did give Monica some more baby Tylenol, so that was good. And I did get a chance to brush my hair.

The Question of Raising Children

It is enormously difficult to talk about how we raise our children these days. How children should be raised, and by whom, are key questions to any discussion of the renewal of culture, but just try bringing up the debate about stay-at-home mothers versus "working mothers" (by which is meant women who work outside the home, leaving the child care to others). Usually it is impossible to get as far as real discourse, because like politics and religion, it matters deeply to us all, and we are, therefore, defensive and cautious.

First, who is the "stay-at-home mother"? Well, the "mother" part means the married woman with babies or small children. The "stay-at-home" part means that she is their primary companion, teacher, and nurturer, watching after them a large majority of the time. Although she may occasionally leave them with someone else, it is her main job during the day. (True, some fathers stay home full time—or split the task with their wives—to raise their small children until they are school age, but since this is still so much the exception, I will stick with "mother," noting that fathers can fulfill this role too.)

Now—before continuing—I am not condemning those parents who must, through force of circumstance, put their children in day care. Single mothers cannot help having to work; neither can the families that would experience complete financial ruin if both parents did not earn a paycheck. But in my middle-class experience, this is rarely the situation. These parents freely choose the two-income lifestyle, and thus full-time day care for their children, for personal reasons, and it is those reasons that fuel the debate.

Beginning at Home

But be that as it may, if our society is to be revitalized, the committed, religious, stay-at-home mother will have to be at the forefront, because society truly does begin at home. The Christian worldview recognizes all people as brothers in Christ, proclaims that where two or three are gathered in his name he is present, and demands preferential treatment for the weak, the defenseless, and the vulnerable. The committed stay-at-home mother has the best chance (and the most time) to proclaim this to her small children each day as she feeds them, bathes and clothes them, reads to them, works with and for them. She proclaims with her mouth what she herself performs, however imperfectly.

This is not to say that families with two full-time salaried parents cannot inculcate a Christian worldview. They can and some do. Yet I cannot help feeling that this way is less efficient, all things being equal, and in the long run less than ideal for children and families.

My suspicion is that a good number of people still agree with this thesis, but a minority put it into practice, and an even smaller minority would openly advocate it for others. Why? In a word, because staying at home with small children is very, very hard: sometimes "battle" is not too strong a word for this life. Perhaps it would be helpful if those still willing to advocate full-time mothering would ponder just what makes it so difficult.

Lonely Mothers

One of the hardest parts is the loneliness. [In the summer of 2002] the kids and I spent a lot of time at the local playground. Because there are no basketball hoops or tennis courts, it is a good place for moms to bring their younger children. It has big old trees around it and a few uncomfortable new benches. Most of us sat at the edge of the sand, taking rocks out of the babies' mouths and hollering at the bigger kids to be careful. I suppose we were all about the same age, early- to mid-thirties.

Amid the chat about the weather (a perpetual topic in Minnesota, even in the summer), movies, and house renovations was a conversation I have heard many times in essentially the same form:

"It's so nice for my kids to have other kids to play with," said one woman.

"You know," said another, "when I was growing up, we didn't have to go to parks very often. We just ran around the neighborhood."

"Yeah," said the first one. "Same with me. My mom just opened the door and we all ran outside, even little ones, four or five years old. We had all kinds of friends on the block and we played outside all day. And all the moms watched out for all the kids. It was safer then."

"It was a different world," I said.

All of us nodded, but no one said what everyone was thinking: it would be at least marginally safer in our neighborhood if there were more parents around during the day.

Neither did anyone point out that fewer women our age are having children, and when they do, those kids are in day care all day long. It was easy to see that we all missed that camaraderie for our children. But it was also painfully clear that these women, just as much as I, missed that sense of community for themselves. It is hard to be so isolated so much of the day. While a person can always get into her car and go somewhere, I find myself wishing for someone to say hello to as I rake leaves. It would be nice, if I got locked out of the house, to have a neighbor who could lend me her phone.

Sense of Futility

If loneliness is one of the hardest parts of this life, then a sense of futility is right up there too. Everyone who has cared for small children knows how frustrating it can be to get to the end of the day and think back on what has been accomplished. True, the stay-at-home mother often gets a lot of things done during the day, her children's needs permitting, but it all begins to look so, well, pointless. Why clean off the towering end-table clutter when it will be back again in two days? Why go to the effort to cook good food when it will be gone in fifteen minutes and, in the case of the children, might occasion unpleasant protests? What earthly good does it do to be here at home when nothing I offer pleases Jonah, when I cannot pitch a baseball well enough to get it near Abigail's plastic bat, and when I am so distracted by the noise and chaos that I find it hard to complete a sentence? At least at my old job outside the home I occasionally accomplished something.

Then there's the problem that comes to mind as I teach awkward Jonah how to put on his shirt (which is harder than you might think when you've never done it before). The average middle-class woman has some higher education, not to mention skills acquired on the job. What will become of all that education (which I am still paying for) once its potency has been depleted by lack of use? Many women need to keep up their skills in order to go back to the workplace, and especially for those women who plan to have only one or two children—in other words, most women in the middle and upper classes—the temptation to keep the skills by continuing to work outside the home is almost irresistible. And working at home, for many people, is a lot harder than it seems, because of children's unpredictability. Even small projects must be accomplished in tiny bites of time: ten minutes here, half an hour there, usually after the kids have gone to bed but before one's own exhaustion wins out. (It took me a month to finish this essay, for example, although I probably did not spend more than eight hours altogether in the writing.)

Then there's the money. Our culture no longer values the household supported by a sole breadwinner. Everything—from buying a house to applying for a college loan for one's son or daughter—seems structured around the two-income family. For example, my husband has a job that pays almost twice the median income in our area for a family of four. Yet when we began looking for larger houses [in 2002], what we qualified to borrow would not buy more than two bedrooms and one bathroom in most of the city, and certainly not in our parish neighborhood. We wanted to buy there because it was safe, with a church, grocery store, library, and post office within walking distance (thus making it unnecessary to have two cars). In the end, we found just the right house—big enough for our growing (and, by the grace of God, large) family—but in a different parish, in a second-tier neighborhood (lots more car theft and somewhat more drug trouble), half a block from a major thoroughfare. This is not a complaint, because whenever I tell acquaintants what we paid for our house (we borrowed at absolutely the top of our range) they are envious. God blessed us with this house and, by extension, with this parish and school.

But not everyone earns as much as my husband. However much women may want to stay at home with their children, they may not be ready to make the sacrifices that it requires. Understandably, they may not be willing to move into a smaller house, in a less desirable location, or to go without a second car, or to give up vacations, eating out, and going to movies.

The Narration Stage

One final sacrifice involved in staying at home is that it can be—what can I say?—incredibly boring. To mention but one example, there is the difficult stage that children seem to hit about age three. I call it Narration. Jonah is currently there and shows no signs of moving on. For those who may not recognize it or whose children skipped over this stage, moving straight from Inquisition to Sulkiness, this is the time during which the child tells stories. Jonah tells stories about the videos he watches. He tells stories about mountain lions, about David and Goliath (in which David's victory is retold and embellished in the most excruciating detail), and about playing baseball. He runs around the house narrating. He narrates on the potty.

More Mothers Are Staying Home

That decision to stay home with a baby for at least a year is becoming more common. A Census Bureau report [in October 2001] shows that 55 percent of women with infants under a year old were in the workforce in June 2000, down from 59 percent in 1998. This represents the first decline in 25 years. The drop is primarily among women who are white, married, over 30, and educated.

Marilyn Gardner, *Christian Science Monitor*, November 14, 2001.

Now these are sweet stories, full of cute malapropisms. But after months of constant chatter, I am bored. It is hard to evoke enough enthusiasm to respond appropriately. ("Wow, honey!" no longer cuts it, now that Jonah is almost four; he wants "And what did David do with the catcher's mitt after Goliath threw it on the ground?")

Boredom is a common objection that many women raise against staying home. They cannot imagine how anyone could stay interested, with no other adults around for eight hours, no real participation in society at large except through commerce and TV.

The fact is, it can be difficult. It seems peculiar to our time that we have so many more ways to amuse ourselves, and so much more time in which to do it. As the average age of American first-time mothers increases, so do the years in which women are independent adults, working but in most cases unencumbered. Pleasing yourself, setting your own routines, always seeking what is interesting—these things aren't necessarily sinful. But they are hard to give up. We have so little experience in enduring boredom for the sake of someone else's good.

A Reward in Itself

I don't know how to solve these problems for other women. It seems useless to protest that, despite everything, staying at home can be a reward in itself. How to persuade someone else that my growing satisfaction with my occupation is anything more than a quirk of my personality?

Yet I wish I could convey it. Like so many other full-time mothers I have learned the obvious: for my children, not just anyone will do. Even the best teacher, the kindest day care worker, cannot replace me, my attentive presence. No matter how closely someone may agree with me and my husband, she cannot guide and nurture our children as we can. No one else can parent our children. It is God's gift to me and to John, ours alone.

If we care about how our country's children are raised, and who raises them, I think this point is where we have to start. And may He who turns the hearts of the fathers toward their children bless all parents, in all walks of life. It is the toughest job we'll ever love.

*"Working mothers give their children . . .
the example of a life lived to its potential."*

Women Should Not
Be Encouraged to Be
Stay-at-Home Mothers

Reed Karaim

Reed Karaim, author of *If Men Were Angels*, argues in the
following viewpoint that working mothers teach their children to be independent, curious, and ambitious. He maintains that children of working mothers do not suffer from
less parental attention than children whose mothers stay
home. Rather, in his opinion, children whose mothers work
learn the value of personal fulfillment and goal setting.

As you read, consider the following questions:
1. According to Karaim, why was the transformation to
   parenthood more difficult for his female friends than his
   male friends?
2. How do working mothers counter popular culture, in
   Karaim's opinion?
3. According to the author, how do most children of
   working mothers feel about their mothers' choice?

Reed Karaim, "The Joys of Having a Mom with a Job," *Washington Post*, July 20,
2000. Copyright © 2000 by Reed Karaim. Reproduced by permission.

L ike many ambitious baby boomers in Washington, most of my friends married in their thirties and didn't get around to having children until that decade was ending or over. They went from being successful two-career couples, happily scaling the ladder of professional achievement together, chatting about work over dinner in Georgetown at 10 p.m., to that sudden, startling state known as parenthood.

A Difficult Adjustment

The transformation was shocking all around (diapers, not dinner, at 10; Gymboree, not the gym, on weekends) but the most difficult adjustment inevitably was for my female friends. Successful editors, publicists, political consultants, women whose confidence and accomplishment had seemed unwavering, were suddenly uncertain about their futures.

How devoted could they or should they remain to work? Were they hurting their children—socially, academically— by pursuing a career? In some cases, soaring professional trajectories were abandoned, part-time arrangements found, accommodations made—out of desire, yes, but also out of fear or guilt.

I understood better when my wife and I had our own daughter, a little later than most of our friends, and began pondering day care. "Of course, it's best if they can stay home with their mother," we heard too many times, as if parental roles had been perfected in the 1950s.

It wasn't as if people were rude enough to suggest this was what we should do. Most were too sensitive, or aware that we needed my wife's income. Rather, it was as if there were an implicit understanding that a mother and child, at home, together, was the ideal situation and all else was, at best, an accommodation, a compromise.

A Misguided Attitude

As the grown son of a mother who worked his whole childhood, I've always been offended by this attitude. Now, as the husband of a working mom, I feel more than ever that it's misguided and damaging. Watching my own wife struggle with her sense that she might be cheating our daughter, watching friends exhaust themselves trying to do it all, I think it's time we both recognize that working mothers have become the norm and celebrate all that they can actually bring to their children's lives.

According to Department of Labor statistics from 1999, 72 percent of all women with children under age 18 work. Even most moms with infants work: 61 percent of all mothers with children under the age of 3. This isn't going to change. [As of 2000, we were] eight years into an economic boom of historic proportions; if ever there was a time working mothers were going to retire from the job force, this would be it. Yet the percentage of working mothers continued to climb throughout the '90s. The Beaver's mom has left a casserole in the refrigerator and gone off to work. She'll try to be home by 6.

What is her family getting in return? For starters, quite often the answer is the groceries and a roof over their heads. The money working mothers make is tremendously important to their families. Two-parent families where the mother works have an average annual income of $63,751, $26,000 more a year than households where only the father works. In most of America, this extra income may not seem extravagant, but it helps boost many families onto the verdant green lawns of the middle class, with all the comforts, chances for education and opportunity that provides to children.

Somehow this gets neglected in the various academic studies that seek to determine whether the children of working mothers do worse than their peers, either socially or academically. The studies disagree. But there's one thing we can be sure of—the money matters.

Setting an Example

Something else that matters is the example we set our children. And one important example is a willingness to work. There's no one who doesn't need to learn this sooner or later, and it's a lesson taught best by example.

If a mother is lucky enough to have a job she enjoys (and, while many of us like to complain about our work, the truth is that most people do like their jobs, at least a little), she provides her children a valuable window into some of the fulfillment possible in adult life.

A working mother can teach the value of independence, first through her own life, and second by expecting her children to take on more themselves. There is struggle in that, yes, but handled right, there can be pride and accomplishment.

Effective Mothering

Good mothering does not require mothers to focus so intensely on their children that they give up crucial parts of their own identities. Indeed, such sacrifice is not even in their children's interest. For if women who are reared to participate economically, socially, and politically stop doing so, they risk their sense of self, their contentment, and, therefore their effectiveness as mothers.

Joan K. Peters, *When Mothers Work: Loving Our Children Without Sacrificing Our Selves*. Reading, MA: Addison-Wesley, 1997.

I know this will upset some parents, but I think the children of working mothers can occasionally even enjoy a valuable sense of freedom. As a teenager, I remember visiting friends whose mothers seemed way too wrapped up in their high school lives. I found myself glad my own mother was too busy to worry about whether I had a chance of being elected prom king. (I didn't.)

A Woman's Value

A working mother, unless she happens to make her living as a swimsuit model, stands as a counterweight to a popular culture that still teaches us to value women more for how they fill out a sweater than a resume. This is obviously important to daughters, but often overlooked is how important it is to sons.

I look at my own mother, who raised seven children while working as a college teacher and librarian, and I think this is one of the great favors she did me. I saw her in charge. I saw her debating things with my father, also a teacher, as an equal, personally, professionally and financially. I marched off into adult life thinking this was the way things were, and I and the succession of female bosses I've had all had our lives made easier.

Finally, successful working mothers give their children

one of the best gifts any parent can, the example of a life lived to its potential. Ambition and achievement are contagious, and we all need role models to encourage our dreams.

This is not to say it's easy, or to dismiss the understandable difficulty of leaving a child and going back to work, or to suggest that our society couldn't do more to support working parents. Nor is it to say that mothers who stay home with their children are limiting themselves; there can be rewards and growth there aplenty. Nothing here is intended to disparage women, or men for that matter, who make that choice.

It is only to say that a working mother need not feel guilty. The pseudo-Victorians and Eisenhower-era nostalgics who wonder how this generation of children will grow up without mom at home with them all day are so in love with a sepia-toned still life that they've missed the bigger picture. As a parent, it's the whole life you bring to your child that matters.

Support from the Kids

Children understand this better than we think. A 1997 national survey by Massachusetts Mutual Life Insurance of 800 15- to 31-year-olds whose mothers worked found that 80 percent thought their mothers made the right choice. An even higher percentage, 82 percent, thought their moms enjoyed their jobs.

I knew my own mother did, and as a child it made me happy. The world seemed full of greater possibility because of it: Her interest in books was contagious; the way she enjoyed her days at the library made me eager to get out into the larger world of ideas and people. Did I feel adequately loved? Valued? Of course. But I also knew there were things that mattered beside me, and that they involved work, but they were worth it.

Someday my daughter will be paying attention when her mother comes home after a good day of teaching creative writing, something my wife loves, and will feel that same contagious joy and sense of possibility. She will be a lucky child. Because her mother works.

"We should, at a much earlier age than we do now, take a serious attitude toward dating and begin preparing ourselves to settle down."

Early Marriage May Be the Best Choice for Women

Danielle Crittenden

In the following viewpoint, excerpted from Danielle Crittenden's 1999 book *What Our Mothers Didn't Tell Us: Why Happiness Eludes the Modern Woman*, Crittenden argues that working women in their late twenties and thirties feel unhappy and unfulfilled. Crittenden theorizes that these women were told by their feminist mothers that delaying marriage and family to pursue a career would provide them with the satisfaction that eluded 1950s housewives. According to Crittenden, however, many women have found that successful careers and independence cannot replace their intrinsic need for a husband and children. Thus, she maintains that women should consider settling down at a younger age than many modern women do. Crittenden is the founding editor of the *Women's Quarterly*, a publication of the Independent Women's Forum.

As you read, consider the following questions:
1. What is the "Selfish Heroine," as described by the author?
2. According to Crittenden, when do men make themselves most absent?
3. In Crittenden's opinion, when will a woman understand true dependency?

The modern approach to romance was perfectly captured in an item I came across one week in the wedding announcements of *The New York Times*. It was a short, lively description of a ceremony that had taken place between a twenty-eight-year-old graphic designer and a thirty-two-year-old groom. "I'm fiercely independent," the bride told the *Times* reporter. "My mother always told me, 'You don't need a man in your life. If you believe you need a man, you won't pursue your own goals.'" And pursuing her own goals is what the woman had done in the five years since meeting her future husband at a party in Portland, Oregon, where both had grown up. The bride, who looked like "a sturdier version of Audrey Hepburn," according to the *Times*, "slim enough to wear cigarette pants, but [also] as if she could change a tire or chop wood," dated but finally broke up with the man in order to move to Manhattan by herself. She said, "I never stopped loving [him], but we were doing our own separate things. Sometimes I think you have to do that in a relationship. It's easy to get complacent and not put yourself first." The man, who couldn't stop thinking about the woman, quit his job and followed her to New York a year later. Eventually they were engaged. As the *Times* noted, "While some couples see their wedding as the moment when everything from their bank accounts to their taste in food must merge," the bride would have none of it. "I think our independence has made us closer, because we both bring something to the relationship," she said. "D.H. Lawrence writes about two people in a relationship being like two stars who rotate around each other, attracted by each other's energy, but not dependent on each other." Their wedding took place, appropriately enough, on July Fourth. . . .

The Selfish Heroine

Of course, her attitude doesn't have to be read this way. And it usually isn't. How often have you watched a TV show or seen a movie or read a novel in which a woman is celebrated for finding the courage "to be herself" by leaving a marriage or starting a new career or telling a boorish husband he'll have to make his own dinner from now on? Her actions are not seen as selfish—or when they are, her selfishness is seen as payback for all the centuries of women's selflessness and sacrifice to men. Almost anything she does in the name of her own salvation and independence is justifiable. This rebellious model of womanhood, or the Selfish Heroine, as she might be called, began appearing in first-person magazine stories in the early 1970s and has been upheld by a generation of feminist writers and thinkers since. Virtually hundreds of novels and television movies-of-the-week have recycled the same plot. The story usually begins with an ending—the ending of a marriage. We meet a woman who is thwarted and depressed in her life as mother and wife. We then follow this woman's gradual enlightenment—her "journey of self-discovery"—as she comes to realize that true happiness lies in learning to value and love herself. She will begin putting her own needs first, until her old self is shed, and she blossoms into an entrepreneur or a congresswoman or maybe (if it's TV) a private detective. Newly confident, she'll trade in her insensitive, staid husband for an artistic and sensitive lover—a college professor or, possibly, a sculptor. Or she'll simply strike out on her own—with her kids or without them—to live a fuller, richer, and autonomous life peacefully by the seaside or in a funky downtown loft, surrounded by her own possessions. The modern fairy tale ending is the reverse of the traditional one: A woman does not wait for Prince Charming to bring her happiness; she lives happily ever after only by refusing to wait for him—or by actually rejecting him. It is those who persist in hoping for a Prince Charming who are setting themselves up for disillusionment and unhappiness.

"It is a novel in which the narrator grabs us by the arm and hauls us up and down the block, to one home after another, and demands that we see for ourselves the ways in which, over and over, suburban housewives of the fifties and sixties came to live out a half-life," writes Susan Faludi in an afterword to a reissued edition of *The Women's Room*, Marilyn French's best-selling 1977 novel. "I had hoped for signs of outmodedness, but the same damn problems French identifies are still with us. . . ." You don't have to subscribe to Faludi's or French's hard-core feminist ideas to have absorbed their certainty that domesticity remains a threat to women's happiness. The idea that dependency is dangerous for women, that if we don't watch out for ourselves we risk being subsumed by men and family, that lasting happiness cannot be found in love or marriage—these are sentiments that are not considered at all radical and with which many more moderate women would agree. And while it's impossible to chart these things, I suspect it's this fear of dependence—more even than fear of divorce—that is primarily responsible for young women's tendency to delay marriage and childbirth. . . .

The Model of Female Independence

[Unfortunately, women find] out, on the cusp of thirty, that independence is not all it's cracked up to be. "Seen from the outside, my life is the model of modern female independence," wrote Katie Roiphe in a 1997 article for *Esquire* entitled "The Independent Woman (and Other Lies)." "I live alone, pay my own bills, and fix my stereo when it breaks down. But it sometimes seems like my independence is in part an elaborately constructed facade that hides a more traditional feminine desire to be protected and provided for. I admitted this once to my mother, an ardent seventies feminist . . . and she was shocked. I saw it on her face: *How could a daughter of mine say something like this?* I rushed to reassure her that I wouldn't dream of giving up my career, and it's true that I wouldn't." Roiphe then goes on to puzzle over how a modern woman like herself could wish for a man upon whom she could depend. "It may be one of the bad jokes that history occasionally plays on us," she concluded, "that the independence my mother's generation wanted so much for their daughters was something we could not entirely appreciate or want."

Unfortunately, this is a bit of wisdom that almost always arrives too late. The drawbacks of the independent life, which dawned upon Roiphe in her late twenties, are not so readily apparent to a woman in her early twenties. And how can they be? When a woman is young and reasonably attractive, men will pass through her life with the regularity of subway trains; even when the platform is empty, she'll expect another to be coming along soon. No woman in her right mind would want to commit herself to marriage so early. Time stretches luxuriously out before her. Her body is still silent on the question of children. She'll be aware, too, of the risk of divorce today, and may tell herself how important it is to be exposed to a wide variety of men before deciding upon just one. When dating a man, she'll be constantly alert to the possibilities of others. Even if she falls in love with someone, she may ultimately put him off because she feels just "too young" for anything "serious." Mentally, she has postponed all these critical questions to some arbitrary, older age.

But if a woman remains single until her age creeps up past thirty, she may find herself tapping at her watch and staring down the now mysteriously empty tunnel, wondering if there hasn't been a derailment or accident somewhere along the line. When a train does finally pull in, it is filled with misfits and crazy men—like a New York City subway car after hours: immature, elusive Peter Pans who won't commit themselves to a second cup of coffee, let alone a second date; neurotic bachelors with strange habits; sexual predators who hit on every woman they meet; newly divorced men taking pleasure wherever they can; embittered, scorned men who still feel vengeful toward their last girlfriend; men who are too preoccupied with their careers to think about anyone else from one week to the next; men who are simply too weak, or odd, to have attracted any other woman's interest. The sensible, decent, not-bad-looking men a woman rejected at twenty-four because she wasn't ready to settle down all seem to have gotten off at other stations.

The Greatest Cost

In the long run the greatest cost to women of uncommitted sexual relationships . . . is that the window for getting married and having children is way smaller than one can possibly foresee at, say, twenty-five.

Lisa Schiffren, *Women's Quarterly*, Spring 1999.

Or, as it may be, a woman might find herself caught in a relationship that doesn't seem to be going anywhere or living with a man she doesn't want to marry. Or if she does want to marry the man she lives with, she may find herself in the opposite situation from the woman in *The New York Times:* Maybe the man she loves has taken at face value her insistence that nothing is more important to her than her independence. He's utterly bewildered by—or resentful of—her sudden demand for a wedding. Hasn't *she* always said a piece of paper shouldn't matter between two people who love each other? And because they are now living a quasi-married existence, she has no power to pressure him into marriage except by moving out—which will be messy and difficult, and might backfire. Whatever her circumstances, the single woman will suddenly feel trapped—trapped by her own past words and actions—at the moment other desires begin to thrust themselves upon her. . . .

The Cruelty of Singleness

Alas, it is usually at precisely this moment—when a single woman looks up from her work and realizes she's ready to take on family life—that men make themselves most absent. This is when the cruelty of her singleness really sets in, when she becomes aware of the fine print in the unwritten bargain she has cut with the opposite sex. Men will outlast her. Men, particularly successful men, will be attractive and virile into their fifties. *They* can start families whenever they feel like it. So long as a woman was willing to play a man's game at dating—playing the field, holding men to no expectations of permanent commitment—men would be around; they would even live with her! But the moment she began exuding that desire for something more permanent, they'd vanish. I suspect that few things are more off-putting to a man eating dinner than to notice that the woman across the table is looking at him more hungrily than at the food on her plate—and she is not hungry for his body but for his whole life. . . .

This disparity in sexual staying power is something feminists rather recklessly overlooked when they urged women to abandon marriage and domesticity in favor of autonomy and self-fulfillment outside the home. The generation of women that embraced the feminist idealization of independence may have caused havoc by walking away from their marriages and families, but they could do so having established in their own mind that these were not the lives they wanted to lead: Those women at least *had* marriages and families from which to walk away. The thirty-three-year-old single woman who decides she wants more from life than her career cannot so readily walk *into* marriage and children; by postponing them, all she has done is to push them ahead to a point in her life when she has less sexual power to attain them. Instead, she must confront the sad possibility that she might never have what was the birthright of every previous generation of women: children, a home life, and a husband who—however dull or oppressive he might have appeared to feminist eyes—at least was *there*. As this older single woman's life stretches out before her, she'll wonder if she'll ever meet someone she could plausibly love and who will love her in return or whether she's condemned to making the rest of her journey on the train alone. She might have to forgo her hope of youthful marriage and the pleasure of starting out fresh in life with a husband at the same stage of the journey as herself. She may have to consider looking at men who are much older than she is, men on their second and third marriages who arrive with an assortment of heavy baggage and former traveling companions. These men may already have children and be uninterested in having more, or she'll have to patch together a new family out of broken ones. Or, as time passes and still no one comes along, this woman might join the other older single women in the waiting rooms of fertility clinics, the ones who hope science will now provide them with the babies that the pursuit of independence did not. . . .

True Dependency

A woman will not understand what true dependency is until she is cradling her own infant in her arms; nor will she likely achieve the self-confidence she craves until she has withstood, and transcended, the weight of responsibility a family places upon her—a weight that makes all the paperwork and assignments of her in-basket seem feather-light. The same goes for men. We strengthen a muscle by using it, and that is true of the heart and mind, too. By waiting and waiting and waiting to commit to someone, our capacity for love shrinks and withers. This doesn't mean that women or men should marry the first reasonable person to come along, or someone with whom they are not in love. But we should, at a much earlier age than we do now, take a serious attitude toward dating and begin preparing ourselves to settle down. For it's in the act of taking up the roles we've been taught to avoid or postpone—wife, husband, mother, father—that we build our identities, expand our lives, and achieve the fullness of character we desire.

Still, critics may argue that the old way was no better; that the risk of loss women assume by delaying marriage and motherhood overbalances the certain loss we'd suffer by marrying too early. The habit of viewing marriage as a raw deal for women is now so entrenched, even among women who don't call themselves feminists, that I've seen brides who otherwise appear completely happy apologize to their wedding guests for their surrender to convention, as if a part of them still feels there is something embarrassing and weak about an intelligent and ambitious woman consenting to marry. But is this true? Or is it just an alibi we've been handed by the previous generation of women in order to justify the sad, lonely outcomes of so many lives?

What we rarely hear—or perhaps are too fearful to admit—is how *liberating* marriage can actually be. As nerve-racking as making the decision can be, it is also an enormous relief once it is made. The moment we say, "I do," we have answered one of the great, crucial questions of our lives: We now know with whom we'll be spending the rest of our years, who will be the father of our children, who will be our family. That our marriages may not work, that we will have to accommodate ourselves to the habits and personality of someone else—these are, and always have been, the risks of commitment, of love itself. What is important is that our lives have been thrust forward. The negative—that we are no longer able to live entirely for ourselves—is also the positive: *We no longer have to live entirely for ourselves!* We may go on to do any number of interesting things, but we are free of the gnawing wonder of *with whom* we will do them. We have ceased to look down the tunnel, waiting for a train.

The pull between the desire to love and be loved and the desire to be free is an old, fierce one. If the error our grandmothers made was to have surrendered too much of themselves for others, this was perhaps better than not being prepared to surrender anything at all. The fear of losing oneself can, in the end, simply become an excuse for not giving any of oneself away. Generations of women may have had no choice but to commit themselves to marriage early and then to feel imprisoned by their lifelong domesticity. So many of our generation have decided to put it off until it is too late, not foreseeing that lifelong independence can be its own kind of prison, too.

"If we ask women to subvert their desires for . . . independence to compensate for the supposed inherent moral deficiency of men, it . . . demeans us all."

Early Marriage May Not Be the Best Choice for Women

Jennifer L. Pozner

In the following viewpoint Jennifer L. Pozner challenges Danielle Crittenden's contention in her book *What Our Mothers Didn't Tell Us: Why Happiness Eludes the Modern Woman* that early marriage may benefit women. According to Pozner, Crittenden asserts that by the time a woman believes that she is mature enough to marry, she is no longer attractive to the opposite sex. Thus, Crittenden believes that a woman should marry before she loses her looks. However, according to Pozner, most men value women for more than just their looks. Thus, Pozner maintains that women should wait to marry until they find a partner who can provide companionship, love, and support. Pozner is a media analyst for the feminist newspaper *Sojourner: The Women's Forum* and a commentator on women for the Fox News Channel.

As you read, consider the following questions:
1. How do feminists and antifeminists view men differently, according to Pozner?
2. As stated by Pozner, on what do New Traditionalists blame deadbeat dads?
3. In the author's opinion, why would a woman be better off seeking a job immediately after college instead of waiting until after she has had children?

B race yourself, because I'm about to reveal a shocking truth about feminists: We like men. Feeling skeptical? Not surprising, since antifeminists have spent the last three decades branding women's-rights activists "male bashers," "manhaters" and "feminazis." In reality, though, feminists believe that men have the capacity for compassion, loyalty, decency and respect—which is why we demand no less in their behavior toward the women in their lives. Ironically, when it comes to their roles within the family, feminists have much greater faith in men's potential as attentive husbands, dedicated fathers and loving partners than do many conservative women.

Certainly we give men more credit than does Independent Women's Forum leader Danielle Crittenden in her book *What Our Mothers Didn't Tell Us*. On the surface, Crittenden's "New Traditionalist" treatise appears to be strictly antifeminist—she says women can attain happiness only by abstaining from out-of-wedlock sex and by "modernizing the traditional idea of getting married and having babies when our grandmothers would have, in our early twenties, and pursuing our careers later, when our children are in school."

At first glance, it would seem that her argument stems from straightforward social conservatism based solely on the notion that women are not well-served by professional and social equality. However, a closer look at Crittenden's prescription for female behavior betrays an oversimplification of the differing desires and socioeconomic conditions of women and a depressingly low opinion of the moral character and emotional depth of men.

Robbing Women of Their Birthright

Crittenden asserts that feminism in general, and female sexual independence in particular, have robbed women of "the birthright of every previous generation of women: children, a home life and a husband who—however dull or oppressive he may have appeared to feminist eyes—at least he was there." According to this argument, men are shallow, callous creatures who will never feel the need to commit to anyone, at any time, as long as they can get no-strings-attached sex from sexually liberated young women. Ergo, the feminist quest for independence leads women to an inevitable emotional dead end, because regardless of how much a woman has achieved, she will feel profoundly meaningless without a husband and children. Why, you may ask, are independence and marriage mutually exclusive for women but not for men?

Because, Crittenden insists, since men are handsome and virile into their fifties, their "sexual staying power" outlasts that of women, whose attractiveness will dwindle with their first wrinkle. It is with this dim view of the heterosexual mating dance that she posits women's chances for lasting love: No matter how intelligent, intriguing, caring or witty a woman might be, few men will find her appealing enough to marry once she feels mature enough to settle down.

Of course, she'll only have "less sexual power" to marry a man vapid enough to value her for her youthful sexuality. Why any woman would want to spend her life with someone uninterested in her mind, her heart or her dreams is not a question that concerns Crittenden, for whom the act of marriage (rather than the quality of that lifelong partnership) is enough to ensure a woman's eternal happiness.

Blaming Feminism

The intellectual stance of the so-called New Traditionalists seemingly assumes that modern men as a class are irresponsible because feminism and no-fault divorce have conditioned them to become cavalier about commitment. Americans used to blame a "midlife crisis" when a man abandoned a graying wife for a "pretty young thing." Now, the New Traditionalists blame feminism. They even blame feminism for deadbeat dads! And, their argument goes, if a modern woman manages to manipulate a man into marrying her and fathering her children, she will never feel secure that her husband won't leave her once her perkiest parts begin to sag or the pressures of parenthood become a drag. As Crittenden tells it, "Even a beautiful woman's looks are not enough to hold a man forever; there are always more beautiful or younger or less demanding women coming along. And if a man does not feel like staying, there is none of the old social pressure on him to do so."

So, since shame no longer works, what's a modern gal to

do? According to Crittenden, the answer seems clear: For any woman to transform an eligible bachelor into a suitable and dutiful husband, all women must lure proposals from men by refraining from sexual activity until their wedding nights, effective immediately. "[I]f women as a group cease to be readily available—if they begin to demand commitment (and real commitment, as in marriage) in exchange for sex—market conditions will shift in favor of women."

In other words gender relations, she writes, simply can be summarized by the cliche, "Why buy the cow when she's giving away the milk for free?" As unflattering as this bovine metaphor might be for women who imagine they have more to offer the world—and any potential partner—than the use of their bodies, Crittenden's invocation of this adage is quite telling. When certain seventies feminists derided the traditional construction of marriage as "socially acceptable prostitution," it was this very commercialization of women's sexuality that they protested. Feminists understood then and now that a woman is more than the sum of her prettiest parts, just as a decent husband has merits that extend beyond the girth of his wallet.

At the heart of the egalitarian marriage under attack here is the belief that men, like women, are complex individuals who long for mates with whom they are intellectually, emotionally and physically compatible. If we do not demand more from marriage than simple sexual access and monetary reward, we must resign ourselves to tenuous relationships devoid of mutual interest, love, respect and trust. Yet, here we are again, reading another conservative pundit rhapsodizing about "market conditions," cows for sale and free milk—as if sex and love are nothing more than products to be purchased like so many hot stocks.

So much for "family values."

New Traditionalism

There is nothing "new" about New Traditionalism. If we were all to follow what Crittenden considers "radical," "progressive" advice, husbands would reclaim their role as sole breadwinners and wives would care for children, hearth and home full time. In an amazing leap of faith, Crittenden states that postponing work until the kids are fully grown would benefit women professionally, because it makes little sense for women to start careers in their early twenties when they are "neither old enough nor experienced enough to get anywhere professionally." Let's test this theory: A typical 23-year-old gen X'er named Chelsea follows Crittenden's path and marries at 25, has her first child at 26 and her second at 29. When her second child enters first grade, Chelsea will be 35; when he enrolls in high school, she'll be 43. Leaving aside the twin obstacles of age discrimination and the gender-based wage gap, let's follow Chelsea as she travels through her job search. How much sense does it make for a 35-year-old to apply for a part-time internship better suited to a recent college graduate? And how well will a woman of 43 with no credible work history compete in a free-market economy against skilled employees with two decades' experience under their belts?

Problems with Staying Home

If a woman does stay home, she should be aware ahead of time that her marriage will not remain equal if she has no income, nor will her future be secure should she divorce.

Joan K. Peters, *When Mothers Work: Loving Our Children Without Sacrificing Our Selves*. Reading, MA: Addison-Wesley, 1997.

Despite these considerations, Crittenden insists women who "neglect their children" in day-care programs are "selfish," because she believes women work primarily for emotional fulfillment rather than economic necessity. Further, she writes, "When I hear a (married) woman say that she would like to have a baby but can't afford to leave her job, what she is really saying is that her husband is unwilling to support them if she does."

Working mothers don't "need" their incomes? Middle-class men are "unwilling" to support their families on one salary? Try the word "unable." Every day the business press carries another story about merger mania, corporate downsizing, unemployment and the plight of the average American worker, who has to put in increasing hours for the pleasure of bringing home a smaller paycheck and fewer (if any) benefits. Job security has become as obsolete as Ozzie and Harriet. Ever since men's real wages began to drop in the early 1970s, more and more women began working not only to become more affluent but to keep up with housing, inflation, the skyrocketing cost of college and, often, to keep their families above the poverty line. It not only is socially regressive to suggest that women must forgo the pursuit of work outside the home—it is an impossibility for all but the most affluent of families (certainly it is beyond impractical for single mothers, widows and the working class). These are the real "market conditions" American women face.

A Crucial Question

In conceptualizing middle-class women's increasing financial need for work, Crittenden asks, "Why have we come to consider taking care of our kids as a perk of the rich, like yachting?" It's a good question, and for women who wish to be with their children full time but cannot afford to do so it is a crucial one. But another question begs an answer as well: If societal help for middle-class women to raise their kids is a good idea, why do conservative antifeminists oppose public assistance to poor women who wish to stay home with their kids? Does it make sense to condemn middle-class working mothers for "neglecting their children" while simultaneously condemning stay-at-home mothers on welfare as lazy and irresponsible?

Which brings us back to the question of the hour: "Is early marriage the best path for American women?" The answer is obvious: If we ask women to subvert their desires for social, sexual and economic independence to compensate for the supposed inherent moral deficiency of men, it not only limits what women can achieve—it demeans us all.

"Feminism is the party of the 'anti-child.'"

Women Should Reject Feminism

Resa LaRu Kirkland

In the following viewpoint Resa LaRu Kirkland argues that feminism has had a devastating effect on women and children. Prior to the women's liberation movement in the 1960s, according to the author, men respected women for their tenderness. However, Kirkland argues that by encouraging women to leave their homes and join the workforce, feminism stripped women of this tenderness and thus of the respect they once received from men. In addition, Kirkland contends, when women went to work, they abandoned their children to nannies and day care. As a result, in her opinion, children today are more violent than they were before the feminist movement. Kirkland maintains that women should resist feminist ideals and devote themselves to their families. Kirkland is a military historian and columnist for *Ether Zone*, an online alternative news source.

As you read, consider the following questions:

1. According to Kirkland, why did mothers in the 1960s begin taking the easy way out?
2. In the author's opinion, what did feminists demand in the twentieth century?
3. What is the goal of feminism, as stated by Kirkland?

Resa LaRu Kirkland, "We've Gone the Wrong Way, Baby: Time for Women to Go Home," www.etherzone.com, May 21, 2003. Copyright © 2003 by *Ether Zone*. Reproduced by permission.

I'm ashamed to be a woman. I feel less for it . . . like I don't quite measure up. Now understand, men have never made me feel less. No, this inferiority complex began about 35 years ago with a little thing called Feminism. Feminism has made me ashamed of my sex—as a group and individually.

There was a time when women deserved respect—because we are mothers, because of our natural softness and tender feelings, because we have been the ones who raised up righteous leaders of good nations for centuries now. *We* dropped the ball on that most vital role, *not men*. Consequently, we don't deserve the respect that men—yes *men*—have bestowed upon us any longer. It is the day care facility—*institutions*—that raises our children now, and the result has been the most horrific social experiment history has ever seen.

The Easy Way Out

In the sixties, women began taking the easy way out. Why? Because Motherhood is a damned hard thing to do. It is 24/7/365. There is no pay, no immediate gratification, little recognition, and more often than not, no appreciation until you yourself become a mother. When you go to work, you get to dress nicely. You have a schedule that you actually keep. People do what you tell them to do. You get to speak to and with adults, have conversations that have meaning. You get regular breaks, and no one is peeing or spitting up on you, throwing tantrums, breaking your things, or calling Grandma to get his way. And while there is truth to the fact that society has both revered and ridiculed that which comes naturally to women—tenderness—it is women—not men—who have inflicted the most damage. Let me explain why.

Men have always been in awe of the female form—not just physically, but spiritually and emotionally as well. While they may burst with pride over their strength and snicker at the physical "weakness" of women when compared to men, they hold in that realm of mystical and reverent those attributes of femininity that are not as comfortable within themselves, and they marvel about them in private moments. They reveal this wondering in ways that are at times misunderstood, but nevertheless bespeak of the awe they feel toward the female sex.

My all time favorite saying about the power women possess was revealed by author Samuel Johnson in the 18th century. *"Nature has given women so much power that the law has very wisely given them little."* Now before feminists start ripping tendons and ligaments with their typical knee-jerk reaction to this example, look again. This is a statement and recognition of the power and strength men recognize within women—power they envy, strength they admire, and tenderness they crave. This is a statement of respect and recognition for women, not belittlement.

Female Histrionics

Jump forward to the 20th century, and the advent of militant feminism that took hold of our culture. Now understand, there isn't a person—male or female—that I know who *doesn't* believe that women were mistreated in the past, or that they deserve rights of voting, work, etc. So let's just toss that ridiculous argument from the get-go. No, this is about the fact that these Stalinistic Types who decided that women deserved better—not just equal—treatment than men have overtaken, destroyed, and even in the face of logic and reason—and their own case studies and evaluations—turned to typical female histrionics to bludgeon society into doing what they say.

This was driven home with a resounding *wham!* when Bernard Goldberg—a man, no less—talked about the final straw that made him decide he could no longer play his part in the Liberal Lineup that has overtaken the media. In his best-selling book *Bias*, Goldberg states that there had been little things for years that had gnawed at his conscience, but it was when he saw what was happening to children—at the behest of *women*, no less—that he knew he could pretend no more.

Goldberg only gave voice to what we've all seen for decades now, but have become too Politically Castrated to say. It is the horrifying trend in our children's feelings, lives, and behavior. You see, when we began giving into the bullying tactics of the feminist movement that used guilt and "Second Class Status" brainwashing to get women to leave the home, it resulted in our children going en masse to day cares or coming home alone. Suicide rates, sexual diseases, poor academics, increased violence and drug use, not to mention less formal criminal behavior such as arguing a great deal, deliberate and even gleeful cruelty, explosive behavior, too much talking, too much fighting have all been the result of the selfishness of the "Woman-Good-Man-Bad" mentality of those who pay lip service only to it being "for the children" when what they really intend to say is "Mine! Mine! Mine! Now! Now! Now!"

Demeaning Femininity

The real kicker to this is that the Gloria Steinems of the world don't even realize what they were saying by getting women to leave the home for the "man's world." It was the women of the world—*not the men*—who force fed women the notion that what comes naturally to men—to conquer the outside world—was more important, better, more deserving than what comes naturally to women. They were actually demeaning femininity by their own words, and were too foolish to even realize it. The shame of my sex is that we bought into it. The shame of the male sex is that they did too.

Feminists and Marriage

• Marriage has long figured as a target of feminist reformers.

• Since the early 1960s, second-wave feminists have campaigned to secure women's complete freedom from marriage.

• The feminist campaigns gave the clear impression that the liberation of women required their liberation from children.

• Marriages must be grounded in the subordination of husband and wife to one another, and of both to the nonnegotiable needs of children.

• In attacking marriage and the family as the wellsprings of civil and political order, feminists are attacking the health of society as a whole.

World & I, November 1997.

Society has paid a dear price for women choosing to listen to these wretched individuals. Women are now in a far worse position than they were 100 years ago; back then, they didn't have many other choices than to be a wife and mother. Today, if they want to be a wife and mother, they can't unless they marry a very rich man. Feminism has enslaved us into the "SuperWoman" role—an impossible place to live. But I have a sick feeling that that is exactly their goal. You see, being pro-abortion isn't enough. They *want* motherhood and wife-dom to be so difficult, so back-breaking, so agonizing in modern living that women will choose *not* to marry and have children. For those who still don't grasp it, let me say it in plain speech: Feminism is the party of the "anti-child."

"Female Empowerment" was the shameful fantasy. Now for the harsh reality. Sisters, your babies are killing each other. They are having babies at younger ages and in record numbers in a desperate search for that unconditional love they couldn't find in the myriad of minimum wage babysitters and daycares they had growing up. They are turning to gangs and drugs to ease the pain of loneliness and the longing for Mommy—a longing which is innate, necessary, and good—and it is our fault. Our children are suffering; their tender feelings have waxed cold and all signs of humanity are dying off in agonizing death throes, and we women are the cause. Women. The givers of life have turned against their own offspring in a vain quest for self-fulfillment. It is madness.

The New Feminist Revolution

Society became this way because we women allowed ourselves to feel ashamed for having children and raising them right, and that was wrong. It's time for the New Feminist Revolution. No longer can our children—or society—abide the general female answer and shrug: "Well, it's the day we live in . . . whatcha gonna do?"

Here's what you're gonna do. Women, go home. Get rid of the huge mortgage and move into a trailer. It's not the neighborhood—*or village, idiot!*—that raises a good child. Have two cars? Get rid of one and deal with the annoyance of having to drive more. It's not the car that makes the family. Fancy clothes and vacations? Trivial and silly . . . those won't be what your child remembers. Be the one who drops him off and picks him up from school. Those precious moments laughing and talking will always be remembered, I guarantee it. Be in the kitchen, filling a warm home with delicious smells, sounds, and memories, and bring the whole family in to make dinner again, cleaning up together afterwards and bonding over pot roast. It is simple, it is time tested, it is true. The hand that rocks the cradle did—at one time—rule the world. The cradle is silent because the hand is at work and the baby at an institution. Sisters, go home—too much is at stake. Your babies are dying and killing, and the only one who can stop this infanticide is you. The power is—and always has been—yours. Take it back now . . . it's almost too late.

Keep the faith, bros—and sis—and in all things courage.

"Feminism has made the U.S. more equal, more just, more free, more diverse—more American."

Women Should Embrace Feminism

Katha Pollitt

According to Katha Pollitt in the following viewpoint, feminism has provided women with many opportunities that were unavailable to earlier generations, including the right to seek an education, play sports, and pursue a career. Recently, however, a burgeoning generation of antifeminists are blaming feminism for many of the problems modern women experience, such as the difficulty of balancing career with family life and the disappearance of chivalry, she contends. Moreover, Pollitt maintains that a conservative government threatens to strip women of some of the freedoms they have won, such as the right to have an abortion. She argues that women need to embrace feminist principles to ensure that women's rights are not lost. Pollitt is an essayist, poet, and columnist for the *Nation*, a biweekly newsmagazine.

As you read, consider the following questions:
1. What examples does the author offer to support her contention that feminism is not a finished project?
2. In what ways do antifeminists blame feminism for many difficulties, as stated by Pollitt?
3. In Pollitt's opinion, how was the pornography war destructive to the feminist movement?

Katha Pollitt, "U.S.: Feminism Lite," *Le Monde Diplomatique*, July 17, 2003. This article is reprinted from *Le Monde Diplomatique*'s English language version, available online at www.mondediplo.com. Copyright © 2003 by *Le Monde Diplomatique*. Reproduced by permission.

The women's movement has transformed the United States in just over 30 years. Stroll through a park and you're likely to see a team of girls playing soccer. Drop in at a law or medical school and women occupy almost half the seats. Women own about one in four of small businesses, and have made inroads in such masculine preserves as bus driving, bartending, the clergy and military—12% of the armed forces are now female.

In private life the rules are rapidly changing: girls and women are more willing to ask men out, and with women's age at first marriage the latest ever, they come to marriage with a firmer sense of who they are; they now expect to work, to share domestic chores, and to have a full and equal partnership with their mates. In liberal communities practices that seemed bizarre a generation ago may be rare, but raise few eyebrows: lesbian co-parents, or educated single women with good jobs, who have babies through artificial insemination or adopt children.

An Ongoing Project

So is American feminism, as its detractors claim, a finished project kept alive only by ideologues? Not so: the rosy picture above is only a part of the truth. Women are still paid less (24% on average), promoted less, and concentrated in poorly paid, stereotypically female jobs. Women working full-time still make only 76 cents for every $1 earned by men. Only in porn movies can women expect to earn higher salaries than men.

Men still overwhelmingly control US social, political, legal and economic institutions and machinery. Rape, domestic violence and sexual harassment are huge problems. In four out of five marriages, the wife does most of the housework and childcare whether or not she also works full-time (and whether or not her husband considers himself egalitarian). The flip side of girls' achievement is the pressure on them from the media, fashion, boys, each other, to conform to a prematurely sexualised, impossible beauty ideal. In schools and colleges, anorexia, bulimia and other eating disorders are endemic.

Feminism has made the US more equal, more just, more

free, more diverse—more American. But it still has a long way to go. The sociologist Arlie Hochschild calls it a "stalled revolution"—in women's roles, hopes and expectations to which society has yet to adjust. Although most mothers, even of infants, are in the workforce, 45% of which is female, the typical worker is still seen as a man with a wife at home, thanks to whom he can be totally available to his employer.

The rules for pensions, social security and unemployment benefits disadvantage women, who are usually the ones to take time off to care for children or sick family. The social supports that ease poverty, childcare and the working mother's double day in European welfare states barely exist in the US: 41 million people lack health insurance; and welfare reform has forced poor single mothers into jobs that are often precarious and do not pay a living wage. Without a national system of daycare or pre-school, finding affordable childcare can be a nightmare even for prosperous parents. It took the women's movement more than 20 years to win passage of the Family and Medical Leave Act, which gives workers in large companies just 12 weeks' leave to care for newborns or sick relatives: since the leave is unpaid, few can afford to take it.

Blaming Feminism

Caught between the old ways and the new, many Americans blame feminism for difficulties. Men no longer give their seats to pregnant women on the subway? Legal abortion has destroyed chivalry. Not married although you'd like to be? Feminism has made women too choosy and men too childish. Infertile? You should have listened to your biological clock instead of Gloria Steinem. The women's movement has never had a good press: every few years it has been declared dead. But demonising feminists is now a preoccupation of ideologues across the political spectrum. On the right, misogynist radio hosts—"shock jocks"—rant against "feminazis", as if a woman who doesn't laugh at a sexist joke is about to invade Poland. Fundamentalist preachers such as televangelist Pat Robertson claim feminism "encourages women to leave their husbands, kill their children, practice witchcraft, destroy capitalism and become lesbians".

The American left, such as it is, is officially pro-feminism, but suspicious of the women's movement—too bourgeois, too white, too preoccupied with abortion rights. For communitarians, feminists threaten the family and the social cohesion married families supposedly produce, and, by focusing on paid labour and individual autonomy, introduce capitalist values into the home.

So much criticism is daunting. It is often said that young women reject feminism. Millions of women under 30 grew up with the idea of gender equality and take their rights for granted. But polls show that they are reluctant to call themselves feminists. "A few weeks ago," wrote Wendy Murphy, a professor at Harvard Law School, "I asked my students (all women) to raise their hands if they believe in social equality for women: they all raised their hands. Then I asked if they believe in economic equality for women: they all raised their hands. Then I asked if they believe in political equality for women: they all raised their hands. Finally, I asked for a show of hands from those who considered themselves to be feminists. Only two raised their hands, and one was a reluctant half-raise." Asked why she avoided the word, a student said: "I just don't see myself as a bra-burning man-hater." Another felt she had been raised as her brother's equal, so had no problems. A third didn't want to limit her politics to gender: she called herself a humanist.

What will happen to them when they enter the legal profession, where 61% of firms have no women partners, 70–80 hour weeks are normal and taking time off for children is the kiss of career death? When feminism becomes a matter of individual initiative—a bra-wearing humanist making her way in a man's world—how does a woman understand and overcome structural gender-based obstacles to equality? Does she join with other women, or blame herself?

Political Correctness

The common European stereotype is that US feminism is obsessed with political correctness and victimology. But PC is mostly a rightwing fabrication, a label that can be used to mock women who object to demeaning or hostile language or behaviour. The US media loves stories about excessive PC—the little boy suspended from school for kissing a little girl, the professor who removed a reproduction of Goya's Naked Maja from her classroom. The reality is usually more trivial and ambiguous than the reports: the little boy, who had a history of disruptive behaviour and genuinely upset the girl, only sat out a party. The professor lost patience with male students who leered at the Maja instead of practicing their Spanish. Even if the teachers acted foolishly, why are these incidents worldwide news?

The Big Picture

Feminism is still needed today to encourage and promote complete equality here and in countries all over the world. Step back from the myopic point of view and look at the big picture. Feminism shouldn't be treated as a noxious pest to society.

Noona On, *Atlanta Journal-Constitution*, January 7, 2003.

It is the same with victimology. The intent is to make those who are disadvantaged and injured ashamed to acknowledge their pain or demand redress: that would be whining, complaining, asking for special treatment. But many women are victimised—raped, beaten, disrespected or discriminated against. When a woman insists on prosecuting her rapist or abuser or harasser, isn't she refusing to be a victim? Are there feminists who will make extreme claims of victimisation? For sure. But they are a very small strand in a broad, even contradictory movement. Since the 1960s American feminism has been fractious and diffuse, encompassing Marxist professors and freemarket stockbrokers; nuns and logicians; lipstick lesbians and Catholic mothers of six.

Feminism is strong in surprising places: among nurses, who have used feminist theory to redefine themselves as holistic healers and patient advocates. While liberal advocacy organisations like the National Organisation for Women (NOW) and Feminist Majority focus on electoral politics, young women put out small counter-cultural magazines— "zines", start rock bands, and organise campus productions of *The Vagina Monologues*, Eve Ensler's hilarious play about women's sexuality, which is performed as a fundraiser at colleges around Valentine's Day.

A debate that seems to have exhausted itself is the pornography war of the 1980s and early 1990s. The brouhaha was immensely destructive to the movement, because it raised questions about sexuality and agency in non-negotiable terms; and it pitted two very American principles with deep historical roots against each other: freedom of speech versus Puritanism. When it came to the idea of women enjoying pornography, two important feminist principles were in conflict: the quest for pleasure without guilt versus humane values like intimacy, responsibility, non-violence, equality. Both sides cited studies supporting claims that pornography did or did not lead to actual violence against women. Intellectually the debate was exciting, but it left bitterness and had little to do with campaigns to protect real women from actual violence.

On the university campus today sex-positivity rules. It is fashionable among young feminists to go to strip clubs, and even work in them. . . . The monolithic, moralistic feminism of the 1970s has given way to a multiplicity of feminisms— queer theory and social constructionism have thrown the idea of woman up in the air. Suggest that a man who's had a sex change isn't really a woman, and you may find yourself tagged as an old-fashioned essentialist.

Feminism Lite

Anti-feminists claim that feminism is a set menu, but it is more like a cafeteria, where each woman takes what she likes. Personal choice seems to be the only value: there are no politics, and no society—to suggest that a choice isn't really free is to insult a woman's ability to know what is best for herself. Having a facelift, which 20 years ago most feminists saw as a humiliating capitulation to sexist standards of beauty, today can be a present a woman gives herself: "I'm doing this for me." The academic focus on parody and performance can reduce feminism to an ironic wink: yes, I'm still in the kitchen, but my collection of 1950s refrigerator magnets means I'm not just a housewife. This is feminism lite.

These internal debates are nothing to the threat posed to progress by the ascendancy of George W. Bush, the Republican party and the Christian right. Thirty years of political and legal advances are at risk. Abortion rights, already threatened in many states, are the most obvious target: new limits are sure to pass at the federal level and in many states as well, and many new anti-abortion rightwing judges will likely rule against legal challenges to them. The Bush administration has allocated millions of dollars for abstinence-only sex education in schools, pro-marriage classes for poor single mothers, and religious-based social services whose aim is Christian conversion; Bush has packed federal panels and commissions with fundamentalists, social conservatives, anti-feminists and other opponents of women's rights. Wade Horn, a key figure in the father's rights movement, is in charge of family issues at the Department of Health and Human Services. Diana Furchgott-Roth, who argues that sex discrimination in employment does not exist, sits on his council of economic advisers. Dr. David Hagger, who opposes legal abortion, refuses to prescribe contraception to unmarried women and wrote a book suggesting bible reading as a treatment for premenstrual symptoms, sits on a medical panel overseeing contraception.

And those girls playing soccer in the park? The Bush administration is considering weakening legislation that requires schools to work toward equalising athletic opportunities for the sexes. Bush-instigated challenges to affirmative action threaten the ability of businesswomen to obtain government contracts,[1] workers to enter non-traditional occupations, and students to attend non-traditional vocational programmes, which are still highly sex-segregated. If these changes happen, will women—those who call themselves feminists and those who don't dare use the word—come together to defend their rights?

1. Until now the US administration had to make a certain number of contracts with companies headed by women.

Periodical Bibliography

The following articles have been selected to supplement the diverse views presented in this chapter.

Paula Adamick   "The Forsaken Feminine," *Catholic Insight*, January 1999.

Anne Applebaum   "Tell the Truth About Babies," *New Statesman*, August 28, 1998.

Patricia Chisholm et al.   "The Mother Load: Superwoman Is Burned Out. Should Mom Stay Home?" *Maclean's*, March 1, 1999.

Danielle Crittenden   "The Cultural Contradictions of Feminism," *Weekly Standard*, July 19, 1999.

Susan Muaddi Darraj   "Understanding the Other Sister: The Case of Arab Feminism," *Monthly Review*, March 2002.

Barbara Epstein   "What Happened to the Women's Movement?" *Monthly Review*, May 2001.

William Murchison   "Revolt of the 'Non-Feminists,'" *Conservative Chronicle*, February 3, 1999.

Phyllis Schlafly   "Understanding Feminists and Their Fantasies," *Phyllis Schlafly Report*, December 2002.

Wendy Shalit   "Clueless: Young Women Are Rethinking the Sexual Revolution. Cindy & Co. Wonder Why," *Wall Street Journal*, May 21, 1999.

Natasha Walter   "We Still Need Feminism," *Guardian*, July 3, 2003.

Lauren F. Winner   "American Girls as We Want Them to Be," *Books & Culture*, September/October 1998.

Cathy Young   "Victimizers: The Right's Confusion About Feminism," mensnewsdaily.com, May 2, 2002.

Tara Zahra   "The Antifeminist Seduction," *American Prospect*, July 1999.

CHAPTER 3

What Should Men's Roles in Society Be?

Chapter Preface

Television is often blamed for portraying gender rules unrealistically, which many experts assert affects how real men and women act. In the past these stereotypes were normally of women, from the perfect 1950s homemaker to the buxom beauties of *Baywatch*. In more recent years some commentators have contended that numerous television shows and commercials have mocked the role men play in society. These analysts assert that instead of presenting men as intelligent and noble, network and advertising executives and writers mock and emasculate them.

According to these critics, situation comedies are rife with plots that denigrate men—in these shows the husbands are frequently depicted as buffoons who could not survive without their wives. Michael Abernethy, the movie and television critic for the Web site Popmatters.com, cites examples from shows such as *Everybody Loves Raymond* and *My Wife and Kids*, where the husbands are often shown to be unable to raise their children or make basic household purchases. *Adweek* writer Debra Goldman also examines this emasculation, observing, "In the fun house mirror of popular culture, we live in a land of blubbery, infantile, incompetent husbands and vital, slim wives who earn half the money but get to spend all of it."

Television commercials have also been associated with unfair stereotypes of men. In an article in *Women's Quarterly*, Ivy McClure Stewart and Kate Kennedy assert that numerous advertisements present an image of men as incompetent slobs who do not know how to cook or shop. The authors express dismay that Campbell's, Levi's, and other well-known brands choose to make men the punchlines to their commercials. Stewart and Kennedy point out that these advertisements do little more than reverse the stereotypes that women have had to deal with in past decades, and they argue that such a switch will not benefit society. They write, "For years, the advertising industry was castigated for portraying women as half-wits, more concerned with vacuum cleaner bags and casseroles than matters of the mind. But, does reversing sexual stereotypes accomplish anything? Who wins when one group is pilloried in order to please another?"

Negative portrayals of men on television could have serious effects, such as lowering the self-esteem of boys and adolescents, who are not shown positive role models. The role of men in society has changed over the centuries as the sexes become more equal, but those changes have not always been positive. In this chapter the authors debate the place men have in today's society. Men's roles are shaped by many factors, including the media.

> "*Fathers . . . take us by the hand, lead us into the outside world, and shape the way in which we confront it.*"

Fathers Are Essential

David Thomas

According to David Thomas in the following viewpoint, fathers are indispensable in the raising of children. He describes how his father's insistence on personal responsibility and respect for women shaped his vision of effective fatherhood. He contends that society holds little regard for fathers, but argues that people should recognize the important contribution dads make to their children. Thomas is a contributor to the *Daily Mail*, a newspaper based in London.

As you read, consider the following questions:

1. According to the report *What Good Are Dads?* how do children with loving fathers outperform children without fathers?
2. What is the feminist definition for fatherhood, according to the author?
3. When did Thomas realize how much his father meant to him?

There is, I think, every chance that Father's Day will be celebrated in our family [in June]. Reminders have been given, hints have been dropped.

So I stand a decent chance of a couple of boiled eggs, with toast soldiers and a cup of tea, being delivered to my bedside, along with sundry cards, chocs, and so forth. Thereafter, of course, it will be business as usual.

A Modern Dad's Job

I know what my job is as a modern dad with two tweenage girls of 11 and 13.

I must stump up money whenever required for sweets, *Friends* videos or Saturday morning visits to [the fashionable clothing store] Top Shop. I must be ready to chauffeur my precious darlings to their many extracurricular events and parties.

And, above all, I must not be embarrassing.

Dads, of course, are automatically embarrassing whenever they speak, wear inappropriately trendy (or un-trendy) clothes, or do anything at all in the presence of their children's classmates and friends. Ideally they should sit, silent and semi-inert, like human mushrooms, doing nothing but wait for their next instruction.

I try from time to time to point out to my offspring that my presence in their lives is, in fact, essential. Why, [in June 2001] a group of four major charities produced a report called *What Good Are Dads?* claiming that children with loving fathers achieve better exam results and are less likely to become involved in crime.

To me that's just basic common sense. But I happen to think that my role in my children's development goes far beyond keeping them in school and out of jail: my own relationship with my father taught me that.

For if it is mothers who physically give us life, nurture us and even shape our basic emotions, it is fathers who take us by the hand, lead us into the outside world, and shape the way in which we confront it.

But you can bet that, even now, hatchet-faced radical academics are trying to come up with research of their own proving that fathers are not only dispensable, but actually harmful to children.

And they will doubtless be abetted by the kind of inter-
fering politicians and bureaucrats whose benefits policies
have actually encouraged young mothers to get rid of their
menfolk and let the State take their place.

Bias Against Men

An entire culture has grown up in which fathers are considered superfluous.

Family law is so grotesquely biased against them that a
man remains in his family home, with his children, on the
sufferance of his partner. If she wishes to be rid of him, he
will find himself powerless to resist.

The father of a family I know well was removed from the
family home because he refused to put up a set of shelves.
His partner decided that this exemplified his inadequacies
and had him out by suppertime.

This institutionalised dadbashing is arguably the single
most pervasive and destructive prejudice in modern society.
And its roots lie in late-Sixties feminism, which decreed that
'patriarchy'—in which men ruled the world as fathers ruled
their families—was the cause of women's oppression and suffering.

Fatherhood, in feminist terms, was by definition abusive.
Grotesquely distorted statistics were produced, purportedly
to show that a vast proportion of men were violent or sexually abusive. Dad, they said, was bad.

Absent Dads

But I'll tell you an interesting and seldom-reported fact
about feminism.

Most of the movement's greatest leaders were not the
children of oppressive fathers, but of absent ones.

For example, Gloria Steinem, the American founder of
Ms magazine—a woman so beautiful she made her name
writing (indignantly) about her life as a Playboy bunny-
girl—was left to care for her alcoholic mother after her
handsome, feckless father left home.

Germaine Greer, the Australian whose book *The Female
Eunuch* was the single most important text of the feminist era,
wrote an autobiographical work with the self-explanatory

title *Daddy We Hardly Knew You.*

The women who claimed to hate the patriarchy had not suffered from its presence in their lives, but its absence.

They felt unloved by daddy, were deeply wounded by his apparent rejection, and this was their reaction.

Dad's Responsibilities

Which all goes to show that a father who has daughters should be aware of his responsibilities, even if Messrs Steinem and Greer were not.

He is, after all, the first great love of his girls' lives, and his response to that love will affect the way they relate to men for the rest of their lives.

For love is a self-fulfilling prophecy. A person who feels loveable is much more likely to be loved. A person who feels secure about giving love will inevitably receive it.

There are, of course, limitations to what a man can offer his daughters by way of practical advice. As they enter their teens—the very time when a father can pass on advice and experience to his son (assuming the son is listening), his daughters enter a realm of which he knows nothing.

Keith Richards, one of my boyhood heroes whom I later had the chance to interview, said that he found his daughters' adolescences baffling: 'You go out on the road for a couple of months, come back, and suddenly Jayne Mansfield's standing there and you're tripping over training bras. That can kill you. They just fling them anywhere.'

There comes a point when girls are initiated into the mysteries of womanhood, and all a man can do is stand to one side and let his wife sort it all out.

But my son, well that's a different matter. For, as my own family taught me, the actions of a father can determine a son's entire approach to life.

The Shared Name

When I was a little boy, there was always total chaos when my grandparents came to stay.

Sooner or later, one of the ladies of the house would call out, 'Da-a-a-vid!' in the way that women do, summoning their menfolk much like dogs.

Seconds later three pairs of feet would be heard echoing round the house.

For, like all the eldest sons in our family, we were all called David.

The shared name has given me a powerful sense of belonging to a line of men, stretching back into time, and forward into the future (My own son may be known as Fred, but he was christened David Frederick.) The family came from Cardiff [Wales], where they worked as millers.

My great-grandfather David was an autocrat and a miser.

My grandfather, David Bernard Thomas, won a scholarship to Oxford University.

Great-grandfather refused to let him go because his three younger brothers might want to go too, and he was damned if he was going to pay to send four boys to university.

My grandfather never really recovered from the disappointment. So when his son, my father, won his place at Oxford, he was given every encouragement.

But my grandfather had the same cussed streak. When my father came home from Oxford and introduced his new girlfriend, a beautiful redhead called Susan Arrow, grandpa was disgusted that she was the daughter of a divorcee.

'How dare you bring that trollop into my house?' he shouted at my father.

Dad laid him out with a single punch.

Susan Arrow became my father's wife—and my mother.

Of course, the fight between fathers and sons is one of the oldest and most profound of all human stories. The son has to shrug off his father's shadow and emerge as his own man if he is to make his way in the world. Which brings me to my own father.

My Tolerant Dad

Reacting against his forbears' prejudice, Dad was incredibly tolerant of my youthful foibles. In the glam rock Seventies, when I was wearing more mascara than Dolly Parton, he somehow managed not to disapprove or even to mock.

I try to remember that when Fred, aged three, parades through the house in nothing but his mother's high heels. Reassuringly, Fred also shows signs of adopting my more macho obsessions, like a passion for fast cars and TV sport.

But I wonder whether he looks upon me in the same way I did on my father.

When I was young, Dad was my hero. Dark-haired, handsome and an athlete, he won the Sword of Honour as an Army officer cadet, got a First at Oxford and was, in later life, the youngest ambassador in the Diplomatic Corps.

He was also my moral compass. I learned from both his qualities and his failings. He was—and at a very hale and hearty 67, still is—an immensely charming, interesting man.

Asay. © 1995 by Creators Syndicate, Inc. Reproduced by permission.

Perhaps because he spent much of his life in Latin America, he entirely lacks the boorishness—the forced jocularity, the excessive drinking, the inability to cope with women— that can be the worst trait of British men.

Thanks to my father, I have never been at ease as 'one of the lads'. On the other hand, as a girlfriend once told me: 'You're the only man I know that I could invite to a hen-night.' I hope she meant it as a compliment.

Certainly, my father taught me to value and enjoy the company of women. He also taught me to take responsibility for what I did with them.

Accepting the Consequences

Dad neither disapproved, nor attempted any nudge-nudge mateyness when I first started bringing girls home. He just told me that if I wanted to act like a grownup, I'd better be ready to accept the consequences of what I was doing.

And then, damn him, he charmed my wide-eyed girl-friends far more effectively than I ever could.

As I became a man, however, I realised that my father was not quite as perfect as he seemed. Or, to put it another way, he had not made the best of the abilities I so admired.

Growing up in a world in which respectability and security were a man's first priorities, he had taken a job that was prestigious, but rarely pleasurable. He was, as a consequence, frustrated.

I resolved that the same fate would never befall me: I would choose my profession on the basis of what would best fulfil and interest me.

But it took more years to learn a deeper truth about my father. He never did anything about his dissatisfaction.

He never grasped the nettle and made a new career elsewhere or seized any of the opportunities that were offered to him in other professions.

By the time I had started work myself, 20-odd years ago, I found this immensely frustrating. As if reversing the roles of father and son, I became angry at him for not making more of himself. If ever there was a time when we fought, that was it.

But fathers never stop teaching you.

The Importance of Family

Now I realise that Dad's apparent lack of ambition wasn't as dumb as it looked. He just knew, before I did, that there are more important things in life than material status and possessions.

Family being one of them.

You only realise how much a father means when he is no longer there. A few years ago, I had to tell my 19-year-old godson that his father, my cousin, had died suddenly.

The poor boy had recently had one of those massive bust-ups to which fathers and sons are prone. It had just about been resolved, but he never had the chance to move on to the more equal, friendly coexistence that comes as fathers and sons grow older together.

Another close friend lost his father two weeks ago, again without warning.

'I always felt immortal,' he told me yesterday. 'But since dad died the clock has started ticking.'

My own father suffered a near-fatal heart condition a decade or so ago. He made a full recovery, thank God. But while he was in hospital, I wrote telling him exactly how much I loved him.

It's Father's Day [in June]. And it is, perhaps, symptomatic of the regard in which fathers are held that this is not usually much of an occasion. But, whatever the politically correct may say, fathers matter, and it's right to recognise that they do, both for society as a whole and ourselves as individuals.

So if your father is still alive, why not let him know how much he matters?

Cards, flowers and boiled eggs are all delightful in their way. But when a father knows he is loved as much as he loves you, that's the most precious gift of all.

VIEWPOINT

"We do not believe that the data support the conclusion that fathers are essential to child well-being."

Fathers Are Not Essential

Louise B. Silverstein and Carl F. Auerbach

In the following viewpoint Louise B. Silverstein and Carl F. Auerbach argue that fathers may not be necessary to a child's well-being. They contend that children need stable, loving role models, and two parents are better than one, but they maintain that families do not have to adhere to the traditional father-plus-mother model for children to have positive outcomes. Silverstein and Auerbach challenge the neoconservative essentialist paradigm that asserts that men and women are biologically and culturally geared toward specific parental roles. They conclude that parenting duties are interchangeable, and that nontraditional households—such as single-parent, gay-parent, and step-parent—can successfully raise children. Silverstein and Auerbach are researchers at Yeshiva University in New York.

As you read, consider the following questions:
1. Why do the authors characterize the neoconservative perspective as "essentialist"?
2. According to the authors, how do marmosets challenge the neoconservative perspective?
3. What is the traditional father-child ideology, and how do the authors want to restructure it?

Louise B. Silverstein and Carl F. Auerbach, "Deconstructing the Essential Father," *American Psychologist*, vol. 54, June 1999. Copyright © 1999 by the American Psychological Association. Reproduced by permission.

In the past two decades there has been an explosion of research on fathers. There is now a broad consensus that fathers are important contributors to both normal and abnormal child outcomes. Infants and toddlers can be as attached to fathers as they are to mothers. In addition, even when fathers are not physically present, they may play an important role in their children's psychological lives. Other important issues about fathers and families remain controversial. For example, scholars continue to debate the extent to which paternal involvement has increased over the past 20 years. Similarly, we are only beginning to study the ways that fathering identities vary across subcultures. Nor do we understand clearly the effects of divorce on fathers and their children.

Overall, this explosion of research on fathering has increased the complexity of scholarly thinking about parenting and child development. However, one group of social scientists has emerged that is offering a more simplistic view of the role of fathers in families. These neoconservative social scientists have replaced [psychologist J. Bowlby's] "essentializing" of mothers with a claim about the essential importance of fathers. These authors have proposed that the roots of a wide range of social problems (i.e., child poverty, urban decay, societal violence, teenage pregnancy, and poor school performance) can be traced to the absence of fathers in the lives of their children. . . . In our view, the essentialist framework represents a dramatic oversimplification of the complex relations between father presence and social problems.

The Essentialist Paradigm

We characterize this perspective as "essentialist" because it assumes that the biologically different reproductive functions of men and women automatically construct essential differences in parenting behaviors. The essentialist perspective defines mothering and fathering as distinct social roles that are not interchangeable. Marriage is seen as the social institution within which responsible fathering and positive child adjustment are most likely to occur. Fathers are understood as having a unique and essential role to play in child development, especially for boys who need a male role model in order to establish a masculine gender identity. . . .

In contrast to the neoconservative perspective, our data on gay fathering couples have convinced us that neither a mother nor a father is essential. Similarly, our research with divorced, never-married, and remarried fathers has taught us that a wide variety of family structures can support positive child outcomes. We have concluded that children need at least one responsible, caretaking adult who has a positive emotional connection to them, and with whom they have a consistent relationship. Because of the emotional and practical stress involved in childrearing, a family structure that includes more than one such adult is more likely to contribute to positive child outcomes. Neither the sex of the adult(s), nor the biological relationship to the child has emerged as a significant variable in predicting positive development. One, none, or both of those adults could be a father [or mother]. We have found that the stability of the emotional connection and the predictability of the caretaking relationship are the significant variables that predict positive child adjustment.

We agree with the neoconservative perspective that it is preferable for responsible fathers [and mothers] to be actively involved with their children. We share the concern that many men in U.S. society do not have a feeling of emotional connection or a sense of responsibility toward their children. However, we do not believe that the data support the conclusion that fathers are essential to child well-being, and that heterosexual marriage is the only social context in which responsible fathering is most likely to occur.

Many social scientists believe that it is possible to draw a sharp distinction between scientific fact and political values. From our perspective, science is always structured by values, both in the research questions that are generated, and in the interpretation of data. For example, if one considers the heterosexual nuclear family to be the optimal family structure for child development, then one is likely to design research that looks for negative consequences associated with growing up in a gay or lesbian parented family. If, in contrast, one assumes that gay and lesbian parents can create a positive family context, then one is likely to initiate research that investigates the strengths of children raised in these families.

Essentialist Legislation

The essentialist theoretical framework has already generated a series of social policy initiatives. For example, a 1998 Congressional seminar that recommended a series of revisions to the tax code that would: reward couples who marry; and end taxes altogether for married couples with three or more children. Other federal legislation has emerged with a similar emphasis on the advantages of marriage. The 1996 welfare reform law begins by stating, "Marriage is the foundation of a successful society." Similarly, a housing project in Hartford, Connecticut now provides economic supports to married couples, and special opportunities for job training to men (but not to women) who live with their families. In 1997, Louisiana passed a Covenant Marriage Act that declared marriage a lifelong relationship, and stipulated more stringent requirements for separation and divorce. . . .

Specific aspects of the neoconservative paradigm have been critiqued elsewhere. For example, V.C. McLoyd has pointed out that families without fathers are likely to be poor; and it is the negative effects of poverty, rather than the absence of a father, that lead to negative developmental outcomes. Similarly, E.M. Hetherington, M. Bridges, and G.M. Insabella have made the point that divorce does not always have negative consequences for children. However, the neoconservative argument as a whole has not been deconstructed. Thus, it tends to be absorbed in a monolithic fashion, buttressed by unconscious gender ideology and traditional cultural values. Therefore, we think that a systematic counterargument is necessary. . . .

Biological Sex Differences

One of the cornerstones of the essentialist position is that biological differences in reproduction construct gender differences in parenting behaviors. This theoretical framework proposes that the biological experiences of pregnancy and lactation generate a strong, instinctual drive in women to nurture. This perspective assumes that men do not have an instinctual drive to nurture infants and children.

The neoconservative perspective relies heavily on evolutionary psychology to support this argument. Evolutionary psychologists cite R.L. Trivers' sexual conflict of interest hypothesis to explain sex differences in mating strategies. Trivers' hypothesis states that, all other things being equal, male mammals will maximize their evolutionary fitness by impregnating as many females as possible, while investing very little in the rearing of any individual offspring. Female mammals, in contrast, invest a great deal of physiological energy in pregnancy and lactation, and thus are motivated to invest a corresponding amount of time and energy in parenting. . . .

The Essentialist Paradigm

1. *Biological Sex Differences Construct Gender Differences in Parenting.*

   The biological experiences of pregnancy and lactation generate a strong, instinctual drive in women to nurture. In the absence of these experiences, men do not have an instinctual drive to nurture infants and children.

2. *The Civilizing Effects of Marriage.*

   a. Because a man's contribution to reproduction is limited to the moment of conception, active and consistent parenting on the part of men is universally difficult to achieve.

   b. The best way to insure that men will consistently provide for and nurture young children is to provide a social structure in which men can be assured of the paternity, i.e. the traditional nuclear family. Without the social institution of marriage, men are likely to impregnate as many women as possible, without behaving responsibly to their offspring.

3. *The importance of a male role model.*

   If men can be induced to caretake young children, their unique, masculine contribution significantly improves developmental outcomes for children. This is especially true for boys who need a male role model in order to achieve a psychologically healthy masculine gender identity.

Louise B. Silverstein and Carl F. Auerbach, *American Psychologist*, June 1999.

D. Blankenhorn and D. Popenoe, like many social scientists, have incorrectly assumed that Trivers' theory is true of all primates, and universally applicable across many different ecological contexts. However, all other things have generally not been equal over the course of evolutionary history. As bioecological contexts change, so do fathering behaviors, especially among primate males.

Marmosets are an extreme example of primates who live in a bioecological context that requires males to become primary caretakers. Because marmosets always have twins, female marmosets must nurse two infants simultaneously. This generates nutritional pressure for the mother to spend all of her time and energy feeding herself. Therefore the father most commonly performs all parenting behaviors. Thus, these animals do not conform to Trivers' hypothesis about the universality of non-nurturing primate males. Marmoset males behave like "full-time mothers.". . .

Another cornerstone of the essentialist position is that the traditional division of labor characteristic of Western, industrialized societies has been true throughout human evolutionary history. Popenoe stated that our hominid ancestors "had a strong division of labor in which males did most of the hunting and females did most of the gathering." A.L. Zihlman, in contrast, has pointed out that for most of our evolutionary history, human societies were nomadic. This bioecological context required both men and women to travel long distances, hunt, gather food, and care for older children and other members of their community. Similarly, in contemporary foraging and horticultural societies, women perform the same range of tasks as men do, and add infant care to their other responsibilities. Cross-cultural research illustrates that women are capable of traveling long distances, carrying heavy loads, and participating in hunting. Thus, the assertion that a rigid sexual division of labor existed over most of our evolutionary history is not supported, either by what is known about human society in prehistory, or by contemporary preagricultural cultures. . . .

The Civilizing Effects of Marriage

The essentialist position has also proposed that marriage has a "civilizing" effect on men. Popenoe, reflecting this point of view, has stated that ". . . all successful societies have imposed social sanctions on men . . . the most important of these is the institution of marriage." Similarly, Blankenhorn declared that "marriage constitutes an irreplaceable life support system for effective fatherhood."

Blankenhorn further asserted that marriage protects women and children from domestic violence. He reported that, as the percentage of men living within the confines of marriage has declined over the past two decades, domestic violence has increased. However, a [1998] report on intimate violence published by the U.S. Department of Justice indicated that, as marriage has declined over the past two decades, so has intimate violence. This report stated that murders of women by their intimate partners decreased 40%, from 3,000 in 1976, to 1800 in 1996. Similarly, nonlethal violence (sexual assault, robbery, aggravated and simple assault), declined from 1.1 million reported incidents in 1993, to 840,000 in 1996. . . .

The Importance of a Male Role Model

Another aspect of the neoconservative perspective is the argument that "key parental tasks belong essentially and primarily to fathers," [according to Blankenhorn]. Fathers are seen as essential role models for boys, relationship models for girls, and "protectors" of their families [as stated by Popenoe]. However, there is a considerable body of empirical evidence that contradicts these claims.

The essentialist perspective assumes that boys need a heterosexual male parent in order to establish a masculine gender identity. J.H. Pleck has demonstrated that empirical research does not support this assumption. Similarly, a significant amount of research on the children of lesbian and gay parents has shown that children raised by lesbian mothers (and gay fathers) are as likely as children raised in a heterosexual, two-parent family to achieve a heterosexual gender orientation. Other aspects of personal development and social relationships were also found to be within the normal range for children raised in lesbian and gay families.

However, persistent, although inconsistent, findings suggest that the negative impact of divorce is more significant for boys than girls. After reviewing the divorce and remarriage research, Hetherington [Bridges, and Insabella] concluded that "the presence of a father may have positive effects on the well-being of boys." These authors also pointed out that the research is not clear as to how father presence acts as a protective factor for boys. H. Lytton and D.M. Romney in a meta-analysis of 172 studies found very few significant differences in the ways that mothers and fathers treated girls and boys. Similarly M.E. Lamb concluded that "very little about the gender of the parent seems to be distinctly important." Thus, the relation between father presence and better developmental outcomes for boys remains correlational, not causal. . . .

Social Changes

If the essentialist paradigm is not supported by empirical data, why has it been so widely accepted? We believe that the appeal of the essentialist position reflects a reaction against the rapid changes in family life that have taken place in the past three decades. Since the 1960's, family formation strategies have changed dramatically in Western, industrialized cultures. The cultural norm of early and universal marriage has been reversed. Fertility rates have declined overall, and age at the birth of a first child has risen across all cohorts. More couples are choosing to live together outside the context of marriage, and a first pregnancy more frequently precedes, rather than follows marriage. Previously rare family types, e.g., single-mothers-by-choice, dual career, and gay/lesbian-parents are increasingly more common.

Industrialized cultures are in the process of changing from a context in which child development could flourish with fathers as the sole or primary provider, to a context in which two providers are now necessary in the vast majority of families. In a survey of 1,502 U. S. families, 48% of married women reported that they provided half or more of the family income. Given this commitment to breadwinning, women can no longer shoulder the sole responsibility for raising children.

In this context of rapid change, the neoconservative position reflects a widespread societal anxiety about "Who will raise the children?" Mothers are no longer at home, and society has not embraced "other-than-mother" care. The U.S., in contrast to other Western countries, has not yet developed a social policy agenda designed to help women and men integrate their work and family responsibilities. Thus, many people believe that a return to the traditional nuclear family structure with its gendered division of labor would be preferable to large numbers of neglected and unsupervised children.

"With the sexual revolution there's been a decline of males."

Men Are Experiencing a Masculinity Crisis

Lionel Tiger

In the following viewpoint Lionel Tiger argues that men have experienced a decline in the last thirty years. For example, he contends, fewer men are actively fathering their children. In addition, Tiger asserts that the number of female college students recently surpassed the number of male college students, and many people have begun to demonize men—who used to be respected for their roles as breadwinners and fathers—as macho jerks. This denigration of men has left young men unsure of how to behave, he claims. Tiger is the author of *The Decline of Males.*

As you read, consider the following questions:

1. According to the author, what position do men constantly jockey for?
2. What reproductive strategy do humans use, as stated by Tiger?
3. What does the author mean by the phrase "male original sin"?

Lionel Tiger, speech to the Independent Women's Forum, July 15, 1999. Copyright © 1999 by Lionel Tiger. Reproduced by permission.

It seems to me that when we consider Aristotle's comment, "Man is by nature a political animal," we all pay attention to the word "political," but not adequately to the phrase "by nature." What indeed is "natural"? You can sell horrible food by labeling it "All Natural," but there is no such equivalent in behavioral terms. It's time to restore some notion of what is natural and to look at behavior as potentially polluted, just as we know the environment can be polluted.

The Relations Between Males

I developed a notion of male bonding because I was very interested in the relations between males—and how males work out a structure within which they can compete with each other and also attract females. Some of you may have been victims, as indeed, I was. Being a small person, I was a ready victim looking through ads in the back of comic books, which offered a 97-pound weakling great dates for Saturday night if only he does the exercises. If I followed the course, then I could kick sand in the face of the town bully. That is a paradigmatic male issue. That's how males are wired.

This is not to say that men have to be savage and mean, but there is constant jockeying among males for position on the basis of which females select the appropriate candidate for their reproductive agenda.

With the sexual revolution there's been a decline of males. One sign of this is that about a third of males are not active fathers of their children. You could say that they have the advantage of putting their genes into the future but get away with not having to pay the orthodontist. On the other hand, parenthood is part of the life cycle in an amazingly complicated way. To not be a father is a sign of real loss for the male.

Reproductive Strategy

That's one kind of loss. The second kind of decline has to do with economics. Women now comprise 55% of the college students in this country. Why? One reason is that women have quickly understood, and so have their parents, that they should assume that they will have to be self-supporting. Greg is not going to come riding around in a Chevrolet by the subdivision followed by a side-by-side refrigerator, so

Susie had better learn how to support herself.

Here comes the concept of reproductive strategy. Oysters and chickens have reproductive strategies. They don't know it, but they do. Humans have reproductive strategies too, even though they may not know it. Susie understands that she may not only have to support herself, but also a child. So she's studying for two. So she is much better at the university system and much more willing to do what is required, than the males.

A Poor Mate

[The] diminished male, some argue, makes a poor mate. His wallet is thin, his self-esteem deflated, his masculinity shrunken. The argument echoes that made since the 1960s by sociologists and politicians about the breakdown of the black American family. With so many black men either out of work, away in the army, locked up in prison or roaming the streets in gangs, black women were hardly spoilt for choice. Hence marriage rates declined, argues William Julius Wilson, a black liberal sociologist at Harvard University.

Now white men too seem to be losing their appeal. In England, according to a recent government report, an astonishing 10% of men aged between 30 and 34 were still living with their parents in 2000, compared with just 3% of women of that age. English baby-boomers of the 1960s are staying unmarried longer than any other generation since that born in 1916, whose marriages were delayed by the second world war. Some of this can be explained by a rise in cohabitation, but not all of it. Women no longer need men even for reproduction.

Economist, December 22, 2001.

How we create positions, jobs, and roles for males is something that we always took for granted. The androgynous commitment to the notion that the sexes are all the same is essentially causing chronic private trauma in countless lives because there is no articulation between the social structure and the real needs and feelings of people.

Male Original Sin

We've been through the First World Sex War. For about 40 years there has been a genuine war between men and women ideologically and symbolically. And males have been defined as having "male original sin." For any problem that exists, it's the male's fault. The males are the principal movers of behaviors that are seen as opposed to the interests of females.

There is an ideological commitment to the notion that any differences occurring between males and females represent a failure of society to create equal and perfect opportunities for everyone so that the sexes will end up the same. This is a mindless concept.

A manager at AT&T called me to help them solve a gender problem. Only 2 or 3% of women wanted to climb up telephone poles and crawl underground to run wires. But the government, the EEOC [Equal Employment Opportunity Commission] people, said they had to have 36% women doing this. AT&T had tried their best but they simply couldn't do it. Finally they compromised with the government. They split the difference. The government said, "You don't have to have 36%. You only need to have 18%." AT&T absorbed the fine, which we're all probably still paying in our phone bills!

It's obvious that so-called Attention Deficit Disorder is a disease in search of a drug company's profit. It didn't exist until Ritalin became available and now 90% of the victims of Ritalin are males. You might find Attention Deficit Disorder in the classroom, but not at recess and not in sports. We're now trying to solve the problem of young males by saying that they're essentially young females. What is happening though is that boys do less well in school and they don't go on to college as often. This will have implications for these young men to be seen as acceptable or plausible candidates for marriage.

Men and Marriage

We know that a child living with a stepfather is 11 times more likely to be killed than a child living with a natural father, and up to a 100 times more likely to be beaten. So if Greg is not committed then Susie has a problem. That's why we have these arrangements like "till death do us part." It's not casual.

The interesting question to me has always been why a man wants to get married. A man meets a woman at a bar, a church basement, or family's gathering. They court for two to three months and then marry, and for the rest of his life, he turns over all of his income to that woman and their children. Now that's really an amazing transfer payment when you consider it. It's really quite remarkable. Why does he do this? Well, he loves them. They're his children. He's defined as an important person. He's got dignified status.

I still remember Gloria Steinem's comment about the ads for laundry soap where the woman would show her husband's shirt and say that the detergent makes his collar sparkly white. Steinem's astute and compassionate observation was "Why doesn't he wash his neck?" Well, he was probably at work all day in a place that wasn't terribly elegant. And he was probably doing quite a lot in order to supply funds to Sue. And most men still do.

That commitment of males to females and to children has been made very tenuous. For one thing it comes back to this war between the sexes. Men who are beer-drinking, football-watching pillars of their little local society, have been mocked and have been treated as macho kinds of jerks. And, so what used to be a family man, somebody who was doing a worthwhile thing, suddenly got turned in a peculiar way into a kind of patriarchal exploiter.

A Peculiar Power

This war against boys or against males has had a peculiar power. Males have become the portmanteau cause of evil behavior and it's acceptable to downgrade males. The impact on young men is that they don't know what to think or how to behave. One consequence is that they're turning to sports. Part of the reason for the intense interest in sports is because it occurs in real time. You catch the ball or you don't. You hit the ball or you don't. There is no seminar about this. Your attitudes and your feelings do not matter. It is a real time event just the way life used to be in the Upper Paleolithic on the savannahs of Africa. Guys like this. It's obviously a symbolic adventure because it captures a deep interest.

So all kinds of things are happening which you can say are behavioral pollution if you will. Or you can simply say behavioral change. I'm not altogether prepared to make that characterization one side or the other. But it does seem to me that it's absolutely vital if we see such change, we should understand that it's not necessarily the result of bad people doing bad things. We have had a very old, animal-tested and brilliant way of dealing with adversity after adversity, for generation after generation. Now, we find ourselves in a very new situation, which is treated as if it were self-evident and it may not be.

"[There is] less of 'masculinity in crisis' than of 'masculinity in retreat.'"

Men Are Not Experiencing a Masculinity Crisis

Deborah Orr

In the following viewpoint Deborah Orr argues that traditional male and female roles—in which women worked inside the home and men worked outside it—are outdated. According to Orr, women's entrance into the workforce has given men the chance to help more with domestic responsibilities, including becoming better fathers. Instead of adapting to their new roles, in Orr's opinion, many men are withdrawing from their responsibilities and blaming women for their problems. Thus, Orr maintains, men are not suffering a crisis but simply avoiding their responsibilities. The solution, she contends, lies in men's ability to adapt to their new gender roles. Orr is a columnist at the *Independent*, a newspaper based in London, England.

As you read, consider the following questions:

1. According to Orr, what is the feminist view of the "male crisis"?
2. What is the primary trouble with the postindustrial view of male/female roles, as stated by Orr?
3. In the author's opinion, what is the "middle-class crisis"?

"Masculinity in crisis" is rather an hysterical call-to-arms, and the banner under which London's Royal Festival Hall is running a series of public discussions involving all manner of men, and one or two women as well. It's a term that gets people going, especially as the very idea of masculinity and crisis living in the same universe are contradictions in terms to any man wedded to the thought that his masculinity may define him.

The Feminist View

The robustly feminist view as espoused by, among others [feminist] Germaine Greer, is that masculinity jolly well ought to be in crisis, because it's such a rancid old construct anyway. The more inclusive feminist view, as explored by Susan Faludi in a recent book [*Stiffed: The Betrayal of the American Man*], is that this is a crisis which women ought to be concerning themselves with, too, and not just because it is impacting on women and children.

The masculine, as distinct from the male view, is that if there is a crisis, it's been caused by women. They have taken men's jobs, insisted they can look after themselves and their children as well, and have used up the nation's health care resources on screening programmes while men die early, horribly and without a soul caring about it. Then they have the cheek to complain when they're 10 months pregnant and not being offered a gentlemen's seat on the train.

All this is, of course, rot. Masculine work such as shipbuilding or steel-working has been nicked [stolen] not by women but by other men. We call it globalisation, and it is not a consequence of feminism.

Women, far from breaking ground in looking after themselves and their children, have retreated, refusing to take full responsibility for looking after other perfectly able adults as well as themselves and the kids. Women patently want more help from men in raising families, not less, which is why it is so very churlish of some men to misunderstand so completely.

And as for women hogging all the healthcare. . . . Well, if masculinity is all about dying of prostate cancer because masculinity is all about never being wishy-washy enough to need to visit the doctor, then it is hardly surprising that a crisis has ensued.

As for offering seats on the train, some men are confident or thoughtful enough to do that thing, but many are simply afraid that they'll get short shrift from some scary lady. Some among those take pleasure in seeing the scary lady suffer. They are the ones who needed the disguise we called masculinity most of all, and the ones who feel the most naked and vulnerable without it.

A Complementary Construct

For masculinity was never much to do with being a man, any more than femininity was much to do with being a woman. Each has only ever been a complementary construct for the other. With the erosion of traditional ideas of femininity, the old ideas of masculinity have also been exposed. Traditional ideas of masculinity are as outdated as the idea that the wife should vote, not just gratefully, but also as her husband tells her. A masculine man was once head of his household, even though he didn't know how many sugars he took in his own tea. Which is, of course, absurd.

It's absurd really as well, to talk about a "crisis" in masculinity. Masculinity isn't what it used to be, that's for sure, and as an identity to hide behind it no longer works. Whether or not this amounts to a crisis depends on how willing people are to adapt. The problem, as I see it, is that men and women are both adapting like mad, but to new models that for both of them are extremely stressful.

Post-industrialisation, the middle class ideal was that a household should contain a woman working within it and a man working without it. This system, if it ever had a "golden" period, didn't last very long at all, because it was so utterly unsustainable from the female point of view. Women were over-feminised, and rebelled against their stereotypes. Men did not, on the whole, join them to question their masculinity. Which is how masculinity reached its "crisis".

Part of the trouble is that the system offers little flexibility. Women, unable to beat it, have little choice but to join it. The sensible new division of labour would have been to maintain the 40 or so hours of outside work in a week, but divided between the two adults. What has happened instead is that it has become the norm for both middle-class women and men to spend a great deal of time at work.

Trading Time for Money

The financial gains that are supposedly driving this double income model, are largely spent on childcare, stuff to amuse the kids, cleaners, gardeners, having two cars instead of the time to walk or cycle to school with the children, and so on. Not to mention the mortgage, and the fact that the more money people have, the more items will cost.

Gender Flexibility

The direction of the gendered society in the new century and the new millennium is not for women and men to become increasingly *similar*, but for them to become more *equal*. For those traits and behaviors heretofore labeled as masculine and feminine—competence and compassion, ambition and affection—are distinctly human qualities, accessible to both women and men who are grown up enough to claim them. It suggests a form of gender proteanism—a temperamental and psychological flexibility, the ability to adapt to one's environment with a full range of emotions and abilities. The protean self, articulated by psychiatrist Robert Jay Lifton, is a self that can embrace difference, contradiction, and complexity, a self that is mutable and flexible in a rapidly changing world. Such a transformation does not require that men and women become more like each other, but, rather, more deeply and fully themselves.

Michael S. Kimmel, *The Gendered Society*. New York: Oxford University Press, 2000.

The idea of workers' solidarity is not fashionable at the moment. But the fact remains that if the will was there for everyone to insist on working fewer hours, and spending more time with our families, then civilisation would survive and thrive under the change. But at the moment, the pressure for part-time work comes mainly from women, setting up further oppositions and competitions within the jobs market.

Men in numbers still cling to the idea that long working hours are bound up with their masculinity, even though this idea is again absurd. Either gender can work all the hours

God sends. It's just that work in the home and family pays in kind not in money. Some of each is better for everyone.

And if this middle-class crisis—plenty of money but not enough time—seems destructive, the impact on lower earners is much worse. In Scotland, the number of female workers has now overtaken the number of male workers, while at the same time Scotland also boasts a high number of single-parent households headed by women, and overall lower pay.

Opting Out

There is evidence here that some men are opting out altogether—opting out of work and opting out of family, leaving a female-dominated workforce desperate to take jobs for which they are paid little. This speaks less of "masculinity in crisis" than of "masculinity in retreat". The inference could be drawn that instead of adapting, some men are withdrawing, blaming women for their troubles, and punishing women and children accordingly. Which is tragic, not just for those men, but for all of us.

For this is the way in which the vicious circle will continue. There has been plenty of venom spread around between the genders over the years in which feminism has fought its corner. I for one have had enough of it.

There are plenty of men who are more than willing to adapt to life in which they have the kind of relationship with their own children that they could not have imagined having with their own fathers. Likewise, there are plenty of women keen to step back from the all-encompassing model of motherhood and give fathers time to parent their children properly.

In the past, from all sorts of branches of psychology, we have heard theories about the pernicious effects of smother love, or dominant mothers, or withholding mothers and so on. The obvious inference to be made from all these observations is that too much of the parental responsibility is falling to the mother, and not enough to the father. Now men have a real chance to redefine their up-until-now rather narrow role in life, and seize the opportunity to enjoy a more rounded maleness than masculinity ever could have offered. It would be terrible if men found there just wasn't the time to really take their chance.

"Feminism is . . . the primary *cultural cause of the current-day bad behaviors of men."*

Feminism Has Harmed Men

Karl Glasson

According to Karl Glasson in the following viewpoint, men have become more involved in crime, have abandoned their families, and are becoming increasingly hostile because of feminism. Feminism, he argues, characterizes men as violent oppressors of women and abusers of children. In addition, feminism has so warped the legal system that women are consistently awarded custody of children, making unmarried men wary of investing in family life, in Glasson's opinion. He contends that men have responded to these attacks by living up to the negative stereotypes cast by feminists. If the vilification of men continues, he maintains, men's behavior is likely to become worse. Glasson is a supporter of men's rights and writes prolifically for online men's advocacy sites.

As you read, consider the following questions:
1. In addition to feminism, what contributes to the problems society faces, according to the author?
2. As stated by Glasson, how have men been portrayed by the gay lobby?
3. What are three consequences of children being raised in fatherless homes, as reported by the author?

Many males in western societies seem to be behaving very badly these days.

They seem to be becoming more involved with crime. They seem to be growing more dishonest. They seem to be increasingly hostile and aggressive toward others. They seem less committed to their partners and to their families. They are clearly doing less well in terms of their education. And they seem to be more pre-occupied with their own narrow self-interests than they used to be.

Why Is This So?

What can possibly account for this apparent deterioration in the behaviours of western men?

Have their genes suddenly taken a dive for the worse?

Or are they simply responding to the way in which western societies treat them these days?

Damning Evidence

In my view, the major cause of what seems to be a significant deterioration in the behaviours of men is, quite simply, feminism.

Indeed, the evidence that damns feminism is overwhelming.

The evidence shows that feminism is not only the *primary* cultural cause of the current-day bad behaviours of men, it is also the primary cultural cause of very many other current-day serious societal problems.

Before demonstrating to readers how it is that feminism is largely responsible for the current bad behaviours of men, it is important to understand the two following points.

1. Feminism—together with political correctness—has been the most influential ideology in western societies for the past three decades. There are no other ideologies that even come [close] to it in terms of the extent to which it has penetrated western societies.

Feminism has penetrated very deeply western governments, western laws, western social services, western universities, western colleges, western schools, western media, western families, western bedrooms, and western minds.

And it has done so for three decades—a decade longer

than even Hitler had—with far fewer resources—in which to stir up his mass hatred toward the Jews.

Feminism has been hugely influential.

And one of its main successes has been the wholesale demonisation of males.

A Useful Weapon

2. Political correctness has been aggressively supported and strongly buttressed by feminists. Indeed, feminists have done their level best to promote any activity which undermines men—particularly white heterosexual ones.

And political correctness has been a very useful weapon for them in this respect.

But the point here is this.

Every ill that can be blamed on political correctness, can also be blamed on those who endorse and underpin it. And no group has done more to foist political correctness on to western societies than the feminists.

For three decades, the feminists and the politically correct have engaged in a wholesale onslaught against white heterosexual men.

White men have been persistently accused of being racist by highly vocal racial activists and racial minorities, and their history and their forefathers have been thoroughly undermined and blackened—to the extent that many racial activists are now demanding reparations for past slavery.

Heterosexual men have been continually portrayed as being violent, abusive, oppressors of women by mainstream feminists and a whole plethora of abuse professionals who have a vested interest in portraying men in this way.

Heterosexual men have also been represented by the beautifully orchestrated gay lobby as being bigoted and fearful of their own sexuality.

All men have been assaulted almost ceaselessly by various women's groups, children's groups, social service workers, therapists, and analysts who have sought to indoctrinate the population with the view that men are abusers of children.

The ubiquitous feminist-fearing mainstream media have consistently sought to demonise and humiliate the entire male gender—a typical example of which can be seen in the

[2003] vindictive column by Maureen Dowd in the *New York Times* entitled "Incredible Shrinking Y."

And the all-powerful western governments together with the legal profession have almost disempowered men completely when it comes to their families, their relationships, and their homes, on the grounds that women and children are often better off without them. ("The Federal Bureau of Marriage?" by Professor Stephen Baskerville gives a good insight into how this is being achieved.)

Turning His Back

In view of all this, is it surprising to find that men are behaving badly?

If A keeps telling B that he considers him to be worthless, and continues to accuse him of things that he has not done, and persistently undermines him in relation to his family and to his children, and continually seeks to portray him as an abuser and an oppressor, who should be surprised if B finally turns his back on A?

Indeed, who should be surprised if B decides to give A a bloody nose?

Well. This is the kind of thing that has been going on in western societies for a long time now thanks to the wholesale demonisation of males by the feminists.

And many millions of men are—and have been—responding to this by turning their backs on their own societies.

Indeed, they are not only increasingly refusing to support their own societies, many are, in fact, responding by giving them a bloody nose!—crime, violence etc.

Well. Let us look at some of the reasons why western men might have become this way as a result of feminism (and, indeed, as a result of political correctness).

Rejecting Worthwhile Values

1. The constant feminist-inspired demonisation and denigration of men throughout the West has resulted not only in many of them feeling worthless, with the result that they now reject the worthwhile values of their own societies (with some turning to crime, drugs, irresponsible behaviours, etc.) it has also undermined any reason for them to shape up.

You might as well be hung for being a sheep as a lamb!

Furthermore, the ubiquitous negative descriptions of men that continually pour out of the mainstream media simply make many men feel quite entitled to behave in accordance with those very same descriptions!

Eradicating Masculinity

The feminists' goal is to eradicate from our culture everything that is masculine and remake us into a gender-neutral society. We see their handiwork in textbook revision and in the constant haranguing by the language gestapo to force us to use such gender-neutral idiocies as he/she. We see this in the war on boys through abolishing recess, overprescribing Ritalin, and the zero tolerance policies that forbid them to play cops and robbers. We see this in the sex integration of Virginia Military Institute and the Citadel, which was a battle *not* for sex equality but to eliminate macho men. We see this in the implementation of Title IX, which is used not to give women equal opportunity in colleges but as a vehicle to abolish wrestling teams and other sports in which men outperform women.

Phyllis Schlafly, www.eagleforum.org, December 2002.

For example, I once saw a headline in a newspaper complaining about the fact that, "Men do not do housework."

As a taunt to my partner, I cut out the headline and stuck it on the notice board in the kitchen. But I added the following words underneath it. "Well, if men are not doing any housework, then neither am I!"

The point is that if men are persistently deemed to be slothful—or whatever—then many men, with much justification, will see no reason to behave any differently from the way in which they and their fellow men are being depicted.

Educating Boys

2. The western educational system has been so heavily biased against boys for the past few decades that they are doing very badly at school. Not only have the educationalists been using diabolically poor teaching methods (e.g., in their teaching of reading skills) but the curricula have been so feminised and politically corrected that boys quickly lose any

interest that they might have had in being 'educated'.

This, coupled with poor standards of discipline, has led to our societies having to bear the burden of having millions of undisciplined, uneducated males in their midsts.

3. The effect of feminism and political correctness in education—e.g., in the study of History—and in the mainstream media, where 'great white men of noble character' are hardly seen to exist any more, means that there are few good role models for boys in their growing years. And the images of men that are daily inflicted upon young men and boys are overwhelmingly negative.

Is it surprising, therefore, that so many men actually have no real concept of what a 'good man' is?

Such men do not exist in the world that is being presented to them.

Shafted by the Legal System

4. Thanks to the wholesale corruption of the family courts and the "no-fault" divorce laws, men no longer have any real motivation to devote most of their lives, their love, their money, etc. into bringing up a family. Why should they—when it can all be taken away from them at the whim of their partners?

Furthermore, prejudicial 'relationship laws'—such as those pertaining to domestic violence and child abuse, etc.—make men feel very insecure within their relationships.

And to add to all this there is the daily carpeting of manhatred that pours out of the feminist-dominated media telling women and children to report their partners for abuse of some sort.

Well. There are only two main ways in which men can deal with the relationship insecurity that all this brings about.

Firstly, they can stop caring very much about their relationships so that they are not too hurt when they eventually break down.

Secondly, they can refrain completely from committing themselves to, or from investing in, any long-term serious ones.

And, indeed, this is exactly what the research shows western men to be doing.

5. The welfare system hotly promoted and buttressed both by the feminists and the politically correct supports single motherhood. And the same is true for the laws concerning child-support payments and alimony.

These not only make fathers and husbands redundant, they also encourage their very own women and children to see them in exactly this way.

Men are, therefore, easily rejected, and they are often also treated with contempt.

They are, after all, redundant.

And another word for 'redundant' is, of course, 'worthless'.

Fatherless Families

6. Family and marital breakdown are the major cause of misbehaviour and poor socialisation in males. Indeed, those who are brought up without their fathers at home are far more likely
  • to live in poverty and deprivation
  • to be trouble in school
  • to have more trouble getting along with others
  • to have health problems
  • to suffer physical, emotional, or sexual abuse
  • to run away from home
  • to experience problems with sexual health
  • to become teenage parents
  • to offend against the law
  • to smoke, drink alcohol, and take drugs
  • to play truant from school
  • to be excluded from school
  • to leave school at 16
  • to have adjustments to adulthood problems
  • to attain little in the way of qualifications
  • to experience unemployment
  • to have low incomes
  • to be on welfare
  • to experience homelessness
  • to go to jail
  • to suffer from long-term emotional and psychological problems
  • to engage only in casual relationships

• to have children outside marriage or outside any partnership

But feminists have always done their best to break up traditional families and to exclude fathers from them, because they believe that traditional families are oppressive to women.

And this particularly huge catalogue of societal ills that has arisen directly from their assault on marriage and family was successfully repressed by the mainstream feminist-fearing media for two decades. . . .

Well, I could go on and make many more connections between feminism and the poor behaviours of men.

But do I really need to?

If you glance again at the [6] points above you will see that they allude to *huge* negative influences that impact, in some way or other, upon *all* males. And they each affect *all* males very badly indeed.

The Main Cause

Furthermore, every single one of these huge negative influences directly arises from ideas and policies promoted and buttressed by feminists.

Indeed, feminism is the main cause of the most pressing problems facing western societies.

None of the above is to suggest that genes do not play a part in the bad behaviours of men. They surely do—just as much as they do with regard to the bad behaviours of women. And neither is it necessary to make any claims about whether children are 'born good'—and are corrupted by society—or 'born bad'—and need to be disciplined and socialised.

The point is that we do know that the way in which societies are constructed, the values that they hold, and the methods through which their aims are sought, have a great bearing on the way in which the people within them behave—e.g., just look at the effects of fatherlessness listed above.

And when an ideology has been hugely pervasive, influential and dominant for three whole decades it should not be allowed to escape from being seen as significantly responsible for the social consequences that are very clearly associated with it.

Furthermore, if western men continue to be persistently

attacked, accused, vilified, undermined and demonised, disempowered within their families, and discriminated against
through the justice system, their behaviours are likely to
grow considerably worse!

And if feminists continue to pursue their aims without regard to the way in which they are alienating millions of men,
my guess is that in the not-too-distant future both they and
their supporters (e.g., in the media, in academia, and in government) are going to be in for a very nasty shock.

Retaliation

Finally, given that feminists have ruthlessly pursued their
aims without regard to the well-being of men, why should
men not now do the very same?

For example, why should men strive particularly hard to
support their families given that some 50% of them will
eventually lose them; and much else besides—with a further
significant percentage remaining in unhappy marriages because they have no realistic alternatives? Why should they
labour to set themselves up for so much serious hurt?

Why should men work for long hours—particularly if
they have onerous jobs and given that the state will take
much of their earnings in taxes? . . .

Why should men commit themselves to one particular
woman when so many are now available for fun and frolics?

Why should men not seek hours of pleasure from superficial pursuits—such as those deriving from their various gad-
gets, toys, sports, and videogames? Do not women spend
many of their hours gawping at celebrities and soap operas,
and thinking about fashion, cosmetics, and romantic fantasies?

Lacking Direction

And what, exactly, are men supposed to be aiming for?

Why should men not be aggressive or offensive toward
women given that women are nowadays aggressive and offensive toward them?

Indeed, why should men pursue 'nobler' aims when these
are persistently undermined by feminists and their governments?

The bad behaviours of men mostly reflect the fact that

western men are now following more their own desires and their own predilections. And they are caring less about how this may affect others.

In other words, they are doing exactly what the feminist handbooks and many women's magazines have been urging women to do for years.

"[Men] can choose who they want to be and what they want to do with lives that feminism cracked open."

Feminism Has Benefited Men

Nicci French

According to Nicci French in the following viewpoint, women are better suited to the new job market—which is characterized by fewer jobs requiring heavy lifting and increased transfer of information—than are men. As a result, she argues, men feel displaced and resent feminism for bringing women into the workplace. However, French maintains that feminism has freed men and women to choose what kinds of lives they want to pursue instead of relegating the sexes to predetermined roles of homemaker or provider. Nicci French is the pseudonym of Nicci Gerrard and Sean French, two English journalists. They are married and live in England.

As you read, consider the following questions:

1. According to French, what should men have done in response to the change in job types?
2. What role do many men who have lost their jobs assume, in French's opinion?
3. As stated by the author, what was the purpose of feminism?

Nicci French, "It's Been Tough for the Boys," *New Statesman*, November 22, 1999, p. 40. Copyright © 1999 by Statesman & Nation Publishing Company Limited. Reproduced by permission.

Norman Mailer, that archetypal male writer, the man who named his penis "the avenger", the man who narrowly escaped becoming the second post-war American novelist to kill his wife (the first being William Burroughs), celebrated his 75th birthday [in 1998]. He commemorated the occasion with an interview on American television in which he anticipated a female-dominated world. In the future, he said, there would only be 100 surviving men whose function would be to act as "semen slaves to a planet of women".

There was a note of lubriciousness amid the prevailing self-pity, presumably because Mailer was confident—even in his eighth decade—of being one of the lucky semen slaves. But the feeling that the world has somehow changed is inescapable.

What Are Men For?

If one of the crucial questions of the early 20th century was Freud's "what do women want?" then perhaps one of the crucial questions at the end is Mailer's "what are men for?" The statistics scarcely need quoting. Girls are overhauling and overtaking boys at every stage of education and in every subject. Especially in America, but increasingly in Britain as well, female students are outnumbering male students, not just in studying literature but in medical and law schools. Boys at school have become an educationally challenged group and teachers are attempting to devise strategies to engage these disadvantaged creatures who don't like books, can't sit still and have the attention span of a hamster.

In western society this has been accompanied by a big decline in the (almost entirely male) jobs that involve lifting objects, and a big increase in the jobs that involve the transfer of information, which women are so good at.

Bad education for the majority of boys is nothing new. In the past it was virtually a matter of policy. After all, if more boys had learnt to read and write and count, what jobs would there have been for them to do? Knowledge is power; education opens windows on to larger worlds. They would have read books, organised, protested. Better to let them mess around in class, do woodwork and then send them out into the fields or down the coal mines or on to the assembly lines.

Those jobs have virtually gone, but we're still only half way out of the old system (though, incredibly, there are still large numbers of people who want to go back to a system of grammar schools and secondary moderns, into a world cut brutally in half).

The new jobs are about tapping keyboards and liaising with people and it turns out that women are better at these tasks than men are. What men "ought" to have done in response to this social change was to stay at school and get the skills that are now essential to success in a modern economy and then later, in their personal lives, to adjust the male and female roles within the family according to their particular economic circumstances.

Maybe this is to ask too much. After all, women didn't change in response to new circumstances—the circumstances changed to suit women's skills and they stopped being thwarted, or thwarted quite so much. In the 1950s, girls' [academic] results were routinely marked down in order to compensate for boys' "later development".

Debating Causes Instead of Results

The traditional patterns of male behaviour may have been selected by evolution in a distant past when the job of men was to spend half the day catching a bear and the other half fighting each other to gain access to the most females. Or they may be a matter of culture, handed down from father to son. People debate the causes but not the results, such as the "crime problem" which in any society depends largely on the size of the cohort of young men between the ages of about 15 and 25. If more of them are hanging around on the street, then there is more crime.

The emotional and interior life interacts with the working one. Doing well, having a purpose, achieving recognition—these are things that catch self-esteem and happiness like a hook catches a fish. In losing work and seeing their traditional roles removed, men also lost themselves. Loss is a word that recurs again and again in the new male vocabulary. Part of the process that they are going through now is a process of bereavement. As we all know, bereavement has lots of overlapping stages: numbness, denial, grief, rage.

There have inevitably been attempts at reasserting, or re-discovering, masculinity. In the past few years in Britain there has been a whole culture of male vulnerability—think of [authors] Nick Hornby, Blake Morrison, John Diamond. Their remarkable books may be about football, the death of others, their own illness, but nagging away in the background is the difficulty of being a man in the 1990s, of lacking power and authority.

Holding Men Accountable

Feminists hate men. How do we know this? Because it is repeated over and over in the media and by right-wing politicians and other so-called guardians of the moral values of the society.

If feminists hate men, then it stands to reason that men should stay clear of—or do their best to attack—feminism and feminists.

I have been involved in feminist politics and scholarship for more than a dozen years. I have known a lot of feminists, many of them radical and many of them lesbians. One thing is true of all the feminists I have known:

None of them hated men.

These women want to hold men accountable for their behavior. They often are critical of patterns in male behavior, especially sexual behavior. They want to change society to eliminate men's violence. But none of them hated me. None of them hated men.

Why not? Because feminism is about the liberation of women, not hating men. And in the liberation of women, feminism offers men a shot at being human beings.

Robert Jensen, *ZNet Commentary*, February 22, 2002.

Other men, inspired by other writers, have gathered together to beat tom-toms and sniff each other's armpits; they have rediscovered a taste for watching sport; they rather admire Jeremy Clarkson[1] for being a lad and knowing what a carburettor is. In fact, the New Lad followed so hard on the barely existent New Man that it sometimes seemed as if the backlash had arrived at the same time as the lash, or instead

1. Jeremy Clarkson is an English television star known for his show about cars.

of the lash. Was there a brief moment when men worried about watching football [soccer] as a substitute for engaging with real life—or even helping with the dishes? Maybe, but this was swiftly replaced by a post-Hornby, post-Fantasy Football version of watching football, in which you sit in front of your TV watching the football as you always did, but you're just a bit ironic about it. And, thanks to Sky [satellite television], there is now so much more football to watch.

Nothing New

Maybe there is always a crisis with masculinity. Hamlet spends four and a half hours worrying about why he can't be a man. The particular nineties crisis comes in many forms. What are young men meant to be or do at a time when the most adored masculine role model is that androgynous, smooth-bodied boy-child, Leonardo DiCaprio? Is that why men are apparently willing to pay money for an aftershave called Harley-Davidson?

And if everything has changed so much, then why does everything look so much the same? When you switch on the news, doesn't it always seem to be men in suits walking out on negotiations with other men in suits? People once said that institutions would be feminised by admitting women. Yet one of the most horribly potent political images of recent years was of [British prime minister] Tony Blair surrounded by the new cohort of female Labour MPs [members of Parliament], for all the world like a beaming prize bull at the centre of his herd of docile cows. And so it proved. Well, not literally, but you get the point.

But if there is anything more ludicrous than the backlash against the female threat, it is the attempt to somehow legislate or preach the genie back into the bottle. According to some neo-conservative commentators as well as a disturbing number of ex-feminists, it seems that what the modern, ambitious, highly educated and motivated young woman can contribute to society is to find a yob[2] hanging around a street corner and restore his sense of confidence by marrying him,

2. English slang for a culture of young men known for rowdy, drunken, violent behavior

giving up work and getting his dinner on the table every evening.

Actually, this woman—the modern woman whom so many men feel hostile towards because she seems to have pushed him out of his desk and off his pedestal—isn't having so much fun either. According to a recent survey, women today are often depressed and weary because they work so hard both professionally and domestically. In spite of all the men who queue up in newspapers to write about changing nappies [diapers] and taking their children to the park and struggling to cook fish fingers [fishsticks], women are still the main carers, cooks, school-lunch makers, face-cleaners, homework-enforcers, willing slaves.

Indeed, in this new world, it seems that men, when they lose their jobs, often become the additional child in the family, babied by the woman they once thought they mastered.

What Happened to Fun?

But all of this—all these claims and counterclaims to be the most put upon and sad—sounds so dreary and passive and narcissistically involved, noisy life reduced to the faint, high-pitched buzz of complaint. Where has all the fun gone, and all the burning, cleansing rage? We hear about bleak men weeping on the couch or howling in the forest, depressed and aimless boys, depleted of all self-esteem, burdened women who struggle stoically from the job they dreamed of getting back to the family they dreamed of having, too tired to enjoy their luck.

This survey actually suggested that feminism—which swung open the prison door for millions of women—has made women sadder. Well, so what? Choice is hard. Choice means taking responsibility for yourself and your life. Nobody said it would be easy. Who wants life to be easy anyway—a flat walk on a straight road, and your heartbeat stays steady?

Feminism was always about women taking responsibility, about having choice. The crisis that men face today should also be about choice: they no longer need to be the monolithic creatures that patriarchy demanded. They can choose who they want to be and what they want to do with lives that feminism cracked open. At the moment, struggling out from their shells, they may feel raw, tender and self-pitying. But this change—presented everywhere as so apocalyptic, sperm-count dropping, suicide rising, with men redundant in every way in a culture that celebrates and rewards work and fame—is also a challenge for them, a possibility.

So we return to Freud's famous rhetorical question, to which he elsewhere inadvertently provided an answer. We are made happy, he said, by work and by love. In the past, men have been the custodians of work and women of love. Now we can have both, work and love, together.

Periodical Bibliography

The following articles have been selected to supplement the diverse views presented in this chapter.

Janet Daley	"Progressive Ed's War on Boys," *City Journal*, Winter 1999.
Economist	"Sometimes It's Hard to Be a Man—the Downsized Male: Even Feminists Feel Sorry for the State of Men Today," *Economist*, December 22, 2001.
Cynthia Fuchs Epstein	"Men Adrift," *Dissent*, July 1, 2000.
Susan Faludi	"The Masculine Mystique," *Tikkun*, January 2000.
Debra Goldman	"The Male Ego Takes a Beating: The Post-Feminist Man Is a Henpecked Wuss. How Did That Happen? *Adweek*, March 3, 2003.
Claudia Kalb and Joseph Ax	"What Boys Really Want," *Newsweek*, July 10, 2000.
Harvey Mansfield	"The Manliness of Men," *American Enterprise*, September 2003.
Harvey Mansfield	"Why a Good Man Is Hard to Find," *Women's Quarterly*, Autumn 1998.
Waller R. Newell	"The Crisis of Manliness," *Weekly Standard*, August 3, 1998.
John O'Sullivan	"The Manly Ideal—Gone, but Not Forgotten," *National Review*, July 3, 2000.
Karina Rollins	"Boys Under Attack," *American Enterprise*, September 2003.
Christina Hoff Sommers	"Boys Won't Be Boys," *Women's Quarterly*, Autumn 1998.
Bryan Sykes	"Do We Need Men?" *Guardian*, August 28, 2003.
Barry Van Lenten	"In Search of Today's Male Icons: Where Have You Gone, Joe DiMaggio? Our Nation Is So Over These New Ones," *Daily News Record*, April 17, 1998.
Olivia Vlahos	"Where Have All the Fathers Gone?" *Women's Quarterly*, Autumn 1998.
George F. Will	"The Mask of Masculinity: Is Manliness Natural or a Social Construction That Causes Wars and Sport Utility Vehicles?" *Newsweek*, July 19, 1999.

CHAPTER 4

How Can Male/ Female Relations Be Improved?

Chapter Preface

Forty-three percent of all first marriages in the United States end in divorce. Many of these unsuccessful marriages are known as "starter marriages," pairings between men and women in their twenties or thirties that last fewer than five years and do not result in children. With modern marriages seeming so impermanent, many people have begun to wonder if the way men and women form relationships in today's world is ineffective. Some commentators on marriage suggest that the best way to find a husband or wife may be a particularly old-fashioned approach: courtship.

Until the twentieth century, when automobiles made it easier for young men and women to spend time away from adult supervision, romantic relationships in middle-class families developed slowly and followed specific patterns. If a man was interested in a young woman, he would ask permission from her family to court her. Then the couple would become acquainted gradually and under close watch from friends and family before marrying. Supporters of modern-day courtship believe that forming a relationship in this manner allows couples to learn about each other's values and interests without the pressure of sexual intimacy.

Courtship differs from dating in several key respects. In an article for the magazine *Insight on the News*, Valerie Richardson outlines the rules of modern courtship, including going out with friends and family instead of as a couple, and maintaining as platonic a relationship as is possible, with premarital sexual intercourse forbidden. John W. Thompson, in an article for *Patriarch Magazine*, is particularly firm about the need to keep romantic gestures out of courtship. According to Thompson, "Contrary to its historical corruption, courtship is not the stage for starry-eyed romance but the time for serious-minded investigation. Not until betrothal should a young man declare to his fiancée, I love you." Amy Kass, who coedited the book *Wing to Wing, Oar to Oar: Readings on Courting and Marrying* with her husband, asserts that "good marriages depend on good choices, and choices are more likely to be good if they are prepared by the activities of courtship." According to Kass, courtship gives young people a guide to help them best determine whom to marry, unlike most modern relationships where "the pursuit of unencumbered sexual pleasure is now severed . . . from romance, love, and lasting, personal involvement."

However, not everyone supports a return to courtship. One recurring criticism is that courtship is sexist and patriarchal, as the possible suitor and the young woman's parents make the initial decision to pursue the relationship. Perhaps surprisingly, this aspect of courtship is celebrated by some of courtship's advocates, such as Thompson. He contends that single women of all ages need the structure of courtship and are "deserving of the male protection over relationships that God intended through a father or surrogate parent." Leon Kass, Amy's husband, is also critical of women's ability to choose their own partners, contending that feminism is in part to blame for the problems facing modern marriage. Naturally such sexist views upset many courtship critics, who conclude that these ideas make it unlikely that courtship could make a comeback in today's world, in which women demand equal respect and autonomy.

Relationships between men and women, particularly romantic relationships, are riddled with complications. In this chapter the authors debate ways to improve male/female relationships. Finding a way for the two sexes to form fulfilling bonds without sacrificing their own interests and personalities has fascinated writers, sociologists, and others for centuries.

"Most men and women seek things in a mate that render something like male headship inevitable."

Traditional Marriage Roles Would Improve Male/Female Relations

Steven E. Rhoads

In the following viewpoint Steven E. Rhoads argues that men and women have biologically prescribed behaviors that complement each other in marriage. According to Rhoads, marriages flourish when men are dominant breadwinners and women are homemakers. He contends that while males are biologically and culturally suited to exercise power, women are suited to nurturing children. Rhoads is a professor of government at the University of Virginia.

As you read, consider the following questions:
1. According to Rhoads, why are feminists disgusted by married men?
2. How do men and women define equality in marriage, as stated by Rhoads?
3. In the author's opinion, how can men be persuaded to dominate less in marriage?

Steven E. Rhoads, "The Case Against Androgynous Marriage," *American Enterprise*, vol. 10, September 1999, p. 35. Copyright © 1999 by the American Enterprise Institute for Public Policy Research. Reproduced by permission of The American Enterprise, a Magazine of Politics, Business, and Culture. On the Web at www.TAEmag.com.

Candace Bergen has now admitted what her TV character, Murphy Brown, never did: Fathers matter. Social scientists have never been more sure, because fathers help boys become responsible men and teach girls good men will love them even if they don't "put out."

And when men—even men who have been good fathers—divorce their wives, they usually end up divorcing their children as well. Two leading family experts, Frank Furstenberg and Andrew Cherlin, find that "over time, the vast majority of children [of divorce] will have little or no contact with their fathers." So if we care about the future of our kids, we should care about finding the secrets to marriages that last through "sickness and health," through "better and worse."

Traditional Christian Marriage

These traditional phrases from church weddings might remind one of the traditional Christian understanding of marriage—one where wives "submit" to the "servant" leadership of their husbands. [In 1998] the Southern Baptists reminded the faithful of this Biblical teaching, and feminists denounced it as "domestic feudalism."

Most of the rest of America shrugged it off. After all, androgyny is everywhere. Women fly jets and make up 43 percent of all law school graduates. Men go to hair stylists and wear earrings. To most of us, male headship seems like something from another planet.

But social science research on intact marriages finds that in real marriages, male headship is simply a fact. Most men and women seek things in a mate that render something like male headship inevitable. If we care about marriages that work, the Baptists just may have something to teach us.

Feminists can hardly look at married men without a certain measure of disgust. Men won't do their share of housework and child care. In the typical two-earner family they contribute about half as much housework as their employed wives and less than half as much solo child care.

Most feminists believe men's power in the home comes from their power in the marketplace. In *Ms.* [magazine] one family therapist sets forth her golden rule of marriage, "Whoever has the gold makes the rules." But the overworked wives cited above are already bringing home gold. Perhaps they're not bringing home enough? To answer, we need to know whether women's power soars when they are the big earners in marriage.

Women as Breadwinners

When husbands make more than wives, both say the husband's job is the more important, but when wives earn more, neither spouse says the wife's job is more important. Indeed, such wives are more likely than other married women to leave the labor force or move to a lower position. At home these high-achieving wives attempt to be especially attractive and sexual for their husbands, and they report indulging husbands' whims and salving egos. When husbands are more dependent on their wives' incomes, the husbands do very little additional housework.

Questions of income aside, there are, of course, marriages where women have more power. Do such marriages make women happy? One survey of over 20 studies on marital power found that wife-dominant couples were the least happy, and the wives in wife-dominated unions were less happy than their husbands.

[Researcher] Liz Gallese's study of women graduates from the 1975 class of the Harvard Business School finds that the women have a tendency to "pull back" on their way to the top. One woman who did not do so was Tess. When her career shot past her husband's, he took on most of the child care. On the surface Tess's marriage made role reversal look workable. Tess seemed proud of her job, her son, and her husband. Gallese did not glimpse the truth until she spent time alone with Tess's husband, who admitted he and his wife had almost no sex life, though he would try to "do things to rekindle her interest."

Soon Tess began to seduce other businessmen. Eventually she came clean with Gallese, admitting that she would love to have another child someday but not with her husband. She stayed with him because he was "a wife." "I absolutely refuse to sleep with that man. I'll never have sex with him again."

Feminists will no doubt say they want neither an old-fashioned marriage nor Tess's but rather one in which promotions and relocations come in tandem or sequentially. But marriages in which spouses devote equal time to work, home, and children are very rare and rarer still are marriages in which the spouses are equally successful in all realms. [Researcher] Pepper Schwartz searched hard to find couples where there was at least a 60/40 split of duties on the home front. Her study found that such "peer" couples feel they have a strong marital relationship with intimacy, mutual respect, and mutual interest. But they also face serious problems. Many husbands are unhappy when their careers suffer. There are constant negotiations and compromises, and serious conflicts over child rearing. . . .

The Appeal of Male Power

Ordinary women show the attractions of male power by making the romance novel the most popular form of fiction in the world. About half of all mass market paperback sales in the country are romance novels. The hero in the romance novel is always a man with power; the heroine seldom has worldly power.

In real life, most women do not seem to want equal worldly power. Even professional women want the man to be chief provider, not only because they believe the husband's work is more important to his sense of self, but also because they need their husbands to be successful.

For feminists the news gets worse. Working women say they respect stay-at-home moms more than mothers who work full time. When asked whether the increased number of working mothers with young children is good or bad for society, women of all educational levels think it is bad, and college-educated women are particularly likely to think so.

Finally, most women with full-time jobs do not resent their double shift. Despite the imbalance in housework and child care, the majority of wives think the division of labor is fair. Husbands and wives tend to define equality in marriage as mutual respect, commitment, and reciprocity over time, rather than as an equal division of tasks.

Once we look at what is known of men's and women's natures, it's not surprising women take to domestic life more readily. It may seem remarkable that men marry at all. The marital ideal is about one man and one woman becoming bound in body and soul—sharing, comforting, communicating through good times and bad. But this ideal resonates more strongly for women than for men. Men want more space. Studies show women like to be alone by thinking in a bedroom or office, whereas men are more likely to need real isolation—a long drive or a trip to the mountains. Think also of those frequently solitary and overwhelmingly male pastimes, hunting and fishing.

The Traditional Baptist View

The traditional [Baptist] camp, advocates equality before God, but is committed to complementarianism, rather than egalitarianism. This is the belief that, while men and women are equal before God, they serve him in complementary roles which are not always identical and in some cases ought not to be. These complementarians recognize that there is "neither male nor female" in terms of our relationship to God (Gal. 3:28). But they also recognize the other biblical texts which counsel that men and women possess distinct abilities and callings (such as 1 Pet. 3:1–7; Col. 3:18; 1 Tim. 2:9–3:7). In the home these ought to be male headship (though not domination) and womanly submission (though not fearful servility). Complementarians insist that to be truly evangelical we must confess that there is no contradiction over this matter in Scripture, and to be truly biblical we must affirm both the spiritual equality of men and women and also the distinctions and differences in roles that are taught in the Bible.

Chad Brand, *SBC Life*, September 1998.

Feminists such as Deborah Tannen and Carol Gilligan make much of the male insistence on standing alone. They think society conditions men to be this way. Theresa Crenshaw, co-author of a leading medical text on sexual pharmacology, once agreed but now thinks the source is testosterone: "The 'loner profile' of testosterone is absolutely crucial to understanding what men are all about. . . . Testosterone motivates the male to strive for separateness in ways a woman is not designed to comprehend." Indeed, "It is fair to say that it causes a compelling sexual urge that spurns relationships, unless they represent a conquest or acquisition of power. . . . It makes you want sex, but it also makes you want to be alone, or thoroughly in control of sexual situations—so it specifically promotes masturbation or one-night stands."

Female sexuality usually functions as a means of expressing affection to someone in a committed relationship. Women's sexual fantasies dwell more on romance, commitment, non-sexual caressing, and story line. . . .

The androgyny advocates believe that with different social conditioning, men can be reprogrammed to become fully intimate, communicative partners like their wives. And once reprogrammed, men will gain from the sharing of problems as women do. But the testosterone research suggests otherwise. So too does a study that followed the progress of patients dismissed from hospitals after recovery from congestive heart failure. For women the absence of emotional support in the community increased their death rates more than eightfold. For men it made no difference at all. . . .

Women as Nurturers

The average woman's innate attachment to and skill with babies would, by itself, be more than enough to sink the androgyny project since most men cannot match women in either the attachment or the skill. Mothers everywhere, in all cultures, take care of young children. This seems to be true even in alternative family forms such as communal living groups and unmarried couples.

Feminists talk a lot about the "burdens" of child care and the "sacrifices" that women make for it. Some women do find child care boring and depressing. But most do not. In her powerful defense of homemakers, *Domestic Tranquility*, Carolyn Graglia describes her child-rearing days as an "everyday epiphany of exquisite happiness." Award-winning novelist Alice McDermott sounded the same note in describing how she and her graduate school classmates were transformed by motherhood. The joy of children seemed "too satisfying, too marvelous" to be put in words. But they tried: "Becoming a mother is the best thing I've ever done." "It's like floating in warm milk." "I could fill a stadium with babies.". . .

Women's estrogen facilitates the effect of oxytocin, a substance which promotes touching, holding, and bonding. During pregnancy and nursing oxytocin surges in women, engendering pleasure and relaxation. When male rats are given oxytocin, they start building nests like their sisters.

The effect of male hormones on nurturing is dramatically different. Evidence comes from studies of women exposed to high levels of male hormones in their mothers' wombs. These women have little interest in dolls as children, and compared to most women, they are less attracted to infants as adults. On the other hand, Turner's syndrome girls, who do not produce the small amount of male hormone most women do, show heightened interest in dolls and babies.

Women's keener sense of touch makes them more responsive to babies, and their high, sing-song voices have been shown to be more pleasing than men's attempts at baby talk. Especially pleasing is a mother's voice. Babies hear it in utero, and after birth its sound slows, calms, and steadies a baby's heart.

Given women's greater interest in and skill with young children, it is fortunate that the vast majority of women and men think wives should concentrate on nurturing and husbands on providing. Data on the proportions of husbands and wives who work full time does not accurately reflect husbands' greater commitment to the work force. Sixty-one percent of husbands work more than 40 hours a week, whereas only 24 percent of wives do. Moreover, husbands are seven times more likely to work more than 60 hours a week. And though 51 percent of wives with children under 18 work full time, only 30 percent want to.

Different Reasons for Divorce

These figures do not point to an androgynous future, and if we want strong marriages we should be delighted. The richest discussion of American men and women's reasons for divorce, Catherine Riessman's *Divorce Talk*, finds women divorcing men who do not work steadily at good jobs; in parallel fashion men divorce women when they fall down as homemakers. Philip Blumstein and Pepper Schwartz's major work, *American Couples*, finds exactly the same thing. Women are much more likely to divorce men who are not ambitious, whereas men are more likely to divorce women who are ambitious. Men divorce wives if they think the wives are not doing their share of the housework. Women do not divorce men if the men do less housework than they would like them to. . . .

In marriage men and women get exactly what they want. If you ask men how they would like to be described, they use words like "dominant," "assertive," "independent." If you ask woman how they would like to be described, they say "loving," "generous," "sensitive." But if marriage means bringing together one person with a taste for domination and another with a taste for generosity, we should not be surprised to find that the former is the head of the family.

In marriages women are more accommodating. If husbands think it is important to have a "proper" dinner, again, it is the wives who spend more time on housework. In family quarrels during dinner, mothers are most likely to compromise. Daughters are the next most likely to. [Researcher] Theresa Crenshaw thinks these inclinations go deep: One reason "women are the peacemakers" is their hormonal makeup. "Mellowing them are their relatively high levels of serotonin compared to the male, oxytocin in abundant supply, and estrogen, a gentle, ordinarily soothing antidepressant hormone."

Another reason women are the peacemakers is their deep need for amiable connection. And their most important connections are at home. Women say that family relationships are the key to their happiness. Family distress has more effect on the mental health of wives than of husbands. For husbands, satisfaction in work or as a parent can offset an unhappy marriage. But for wives, feminist Rosalind Barnett and coauthors report that "dissatisfaction in the marital role cannot be compensated for by satisfaction in any other role.". . .

Tempering Male Headship

If any women should still be reading, please note I have been describing how things are. As for how things might be, I would argue for a kinder and gentler male headship. For all the reasons given, the headship part won't go away. Most women don't really want it to. They like a manly man in the outside world and in the bedroom. They could, however, do with men who are a little less lordly in the rest of the house.

And if we care about solid marriages that rear solid children, we have to side with wives here. Riessman's *Divorce Talk* describes women filing for divorce because they feel devalued and dominated. In retrospect even their former husbands often agree they were treating their wives like "a dictator" or "a little Hitler." Although many happy marriages are characterized by moderate male dominance, marriages often fail when there is extreme male dominance. [Researcher] John Gottman finds successful marriages have a husband who accepts a wife's influence. They also have wives who couch complaints in a gentle, soothing, sometimes humorous way.

But how can we induce the stronger sex that likes to dominate to do it less? This is where the Baptists can help, by reminding men of their sacred obligation to use their familial power to serve their families. Husbands must be ready to sacrifice themselves for their wives and children as Christ gave all for the church. By making the male role in marriage vital, Baptists attract more men to it. And by condemning extramarital sex, they make alternatives to marriage less attractive and less available. . . .

Wives doubtful about granting husbands titular headship should realize they may not have to give up much more than the title. Studies suggest husbands overestimate their decisionmaking power while wives underestimate theirs. Indeed, one study found "the most satisfied husbands were those who believed they had the greater decision-making power even where there was no independent evidence of it." Women in such marriages probably rule indirectly as the wisest wives usually do. David Blankenhorn tells the tale of a traditional wife who said her husband was the head of the family and she was the neck—which turns the head in the direction it should go. Most wives set husbands going in better directions, and civilization is in their debt.

"Were marriages between women and men to become truly egalitarian . . . feminists would rejoice."

Egalitarian Marriage Roles Would Improve Male/Female Relations

Janet C. Gornick

According to Janet C. Gornick in the following viewpoint, conservatives misguidedly perceive feminism to be opposed to marriage. Gornick argues that feminists oppose unequal marriage, not marriage in general. She contends that wives consistently sacrifice their careers, take home lower pay, and handle more housework and child care than their husbands. In Gornick's opinion, revising social and employment policies that support this unequal division of labor—such as enacting paid paternity leave and instituting a shorter work week—could improve male/female relations by helping couples divide marital responsibilities more fairly. Gornick is an associate professor of political science at the Graduate Center and Baruch College at the City University of New York.

As you read, consider the following questions:
1. According to Gornick, how do sexual divisions of labor negatively affect women?
2. What two views of equity within marriage do feminists espouse, as stated by Gornick?
3. What elements of Gornick's proposed policy package will appeal to conservatives, in her opinion?

Feminists have long been queasy about marriage, but our queasiness is not about marriage per se; it concerns the way marriage has been practiced. The religious right paints feminists as opposed to marriage and all that goes with it: heterosexuality, men, family, love, caring, and children. Campaigning against the Equal Rights Amendment in the 1970s, Phyllis Schlafly flatly warned that "feminists hate men, marriage, and children." Twenty years later, Pat Robertson advised would-be supporters in a fundraising letter: "The feminist agenda is not about equal rights for women. It is about a socialist, anti-family political movement that encourages women to leave their husbands, kill their children . . . and become lesbians."

Battling for Egalitarian Marriage

Clearly, the right misrepresents feminists' struggle with marriage, but many moderates and even some progressives have misunderstood feminist concerns. What have American feminists really said about marriage? During the first wave of the American women's movement, which intensified during the 1840s and culminated with the achievement of suffrage in 1920, feminists battled for egalitarian marriage as passionately as they fought for voting rights. In 1848—in the Declaration of Sentiments adopted at the First Women's Rights Convention at Seneca Falls, New York—Mary Ann McClintock and Elizabeth Cady Stanton wrote:

> The history of mankind is a history of repeated injuries and usurpations on the part of man toward woman. . . . He has made her, if married, in the eye of the law, civilly dead. He has taken from her all right in property, even to the wages she earns. . . . In the covenant of marriage, . . . the law gives him power to deprive her of her liberty and to administer chastisement.

For the most part, nineteenth-century feminists did not oppose marriage itself. Rather, they fought tirelessly for the legal rights of wives, gradually winning statutory reforms that granted married women property rights.

A second wave of American feminism emerged in the 1960s, catalyzed in part by Betty Friedan's 1963 book *The Feminine Mystique*, which sparked a nationwide soul-search about the emptiness of housewifery. "It was a strange stirring, a sense of dissatisfaction, a yearning," Friedan wrote. "As [each suburban housewife] made the beds, shopped for groceries, matched slip cover materials, ate peanut butter sandwiches with her children, chauffeured Cub Scouts and Brownies . . . she was afraid to ask of herself the silent question—'Is this all?'" Friedan's book pulled countless wives into the women's movement and dovetailed with activist efforts aimed at breaking down employment barriers.

While the legal constraints that galvanized their predecessors a century earlier were mostly gone, the new women's liberationists found that marriage, de facto, still served many women poorly, especially in conjunction with motherhood. Sexual divisions of labor, locked in by the social norms of marriage, yielded gender inequality both in the labor market and the home, saddling women with the lion's share of housework. Those divisions of labor institutionalized wives' economic dependence on their husbands; in the worst scenarios, that dependence placed women in outright danger. Furthermore, feminists argued, the centrality of marriage in the dreams and expectations of girls and young women crowded out long-term aspirations for education, employment, and civic and political engagement.

Those were the central feminist concerns about marriage nearly four decades ago, and they are still the central feminist concerns today. Pegging feminists as coldhearted haters of heterosexuality, love, care, and commitment has always been a bum rap. Were marriages between women and men to become truly egalitarian—especially in economic terms—most contemporary feminists would rejoice. Were same-sex couples invited to participate, feminism and marriage could announce a full truce. . . .

Unequal Marriage: The Price Women Pay

Today, a small minority of couples consist of an exclusive male breadwinner and a full-time female homemaker; in most marriages, husband and wife are both employed. However, the labor-force attachment of husbands remains considerably stronger, especially in families with children; very few men are on a career-sacrificing "daddy track." Married mothers often withdraw from paid work when their children are young; many more work part-time; and a substantial share forgo remunerative jobs that require "24-7" commitment, nighttime meetings, or travel. Few married fathers make such accommodations to family. Not surprisingly, despite progress in women's employment, men remain the primary breadwinners. As of 1997, among American married couples with children under age six, fathers took home three times the earnings of mothers. And studies confirm that wives, even wives employed full-time, still devote substantially more time than their husbands do to unpaid work—both caregiving and housework.

Certainly, children need and deserve their parents' time. It's appropriate that parents weaken labor-market ties when their children are young. The trouble, however, is that marital divisions of labor shape up along gender lines, there are hazards associated with being the non-earner or lower earner, and those hazards are very unequally distributed.

Non-earners (and lower earners) in intact couples lack bargaining power both in the economy and in the marriage. And the lower-earning partner is financially vulnerable in the event of marital dissolution, despite divorce and child-support laws intended to protect them. In addition, weak labor-market ties often mean tenuous civic and political ties which translate into compromised power both inside and outside the home. In his 2000 book *Bowling Alone*, Robert D. Putnam contradicts the old picture of housewives as pillars of local civil society and links women's connections to employment to their participation in public forms of civic engagement.

Another problem: Huge numbers of married women are plain exhausted, battling worse "time poverty" than their husbands, particularly if they have young children and are also in paid employment. And where are the fruits of wives' unpaid work? One place is in their husbands' wages. A recent study reported in *BusinessWeek* found that wives' unpaid work raises married men's hourly wages by about 12 percent—a "marriage premium" for men that is explained by the "likelihood that wives shoulder household tasks." Women, meanwhile, suffer reduced earnings, not because of marriage per se, but owing to the presence of children. And nearly two-thirds of married women have children. As Ann Crittenden establishes in *The Price of Motherhood*, because of their family responsibilities women in effect pay a hefty "mommy tax" on their earnings—a tax not incurred by their children's daddies.

In their much-argued-about book *The Case for Marriage: Why Married People Are Happier, Healthier, and Better Off Financially*, Linda Waite and Maggie Gallagher dismiss most of these concerns. Wives, they argue, are simply better off financially because they have access to their husbands' (increased) income as well as their own (albeit diminished) income; the two together add up to more than she would have had living alone or cohabiting. As for wives' economic dependency on their husbands, Waite and Gallagher are largely unmoved. (I suspected that when, on page 1, they characterized the women's movement as criticizing "marriage per se, which the more flamboyant feminists denounced as, . . . worst of all, 'tied up with a sense of dependency.'") For the most part, these writers view the underlying economic inequality as the result of women's choices—"married moms earn less because they choose to work less"—but they don't seriously consider whether those supposed free choices are constrained by the absence of good alternatives that is inherent in archaic notions about gender, inflexible employment practices, and unsupportive public policies. In the end, they argue that making divorce more difficult and enacting divorce laws that repay women for the sacrificed labor-market attachment can indemnify wives against any losses that they incur. Fairer divorce laws are fine—but why wait for marriages to end? For all their advocacy of marriage, Waite and Gallagher leave untouched the underlying inequities that make marriage costly for so many women.

Toward Egalitarian Marriage

Among feminists, there are two broad views about greater equity within marriage. "Difference feminists" argue that women's unique characteristics, such as their stronger ties to children, should be celebrated and rewarded. From this perspective, gender equity would be achieved by making parenting a less-unequal sacrifice; essentially, wives would be repaid for the losses that they incur as individuals. "Sameness feminists," by contrast, look toward a greater convergence in gender roles—a rearrangement of marital divisions of labor so that on average wives and husbands, in Francine Deutsch's phrase, would "halve it all."

Gibbons. © by Anne Gibbons. Reproduced by permission.

The latter approach seems more promising. Reliably indemnifying women against losses caused by their greater role in family caregiving is improbable because it is so easy for husbands, employers, and even governments to free-ride on women's unpaid work. And any solution that continues gendered divisions of labor leaves in place problematic power imbalances, both public and private.

Across Europe, feminists have taken seriously this idea of greater convergence of roles in the workplace and the home. In her recent book *Restructuring Gender Relations and Employ-*

ment: The Decline of the Male Breadwinner, British sociologist Rosemary Crompton lays out the contours of what she calls a "dual-earner/dual-carer" society. This is a society in which women and men engage symmetrically in market work and in caregiving work—a society that incorporates time to care for family members. Wives would not simply become "like husbands are now"; both wives and husbands would end up with substantial time for caregiving at home. . . .

An egalitarian solution would entail both parents working a slightly-shorter-than-standard workweek and sharing caregiving in the home. In principle this might seem appealing to men, who often say they are sick of employment pressures, want more balance in their lives, and hope to be better fathers than their own fathers were. But for this solution to be attractive to both sexes, workplace practices have to change so that neither spouse suffers a setback as the result of caring for children. And social policy also has to change—starting with, for example, the enactment of generous paid family leave for both fathers and mothers. . . .

Supportive Public Policy

How might we get from here to there? As European feminists painted portraits of the dual-earner/dual-carer society, they also envisioned a change process. Clearly, private changes in gender relations and shifts in employment practices are part of the story; but the state also plays a crucial role, both in shaping social policy and regulating labor markets.

Couples' capacity to choose egalitarian arrangements would be facilitated by a package of government policies, many of which are in place across the European welfare states. A supportive policy package would have at least four aims: to enable and support the employment of mothers with young children; to provide incentives for men to engage in caregiving at home; to support the development of high-quality reduced-hour work for both mothers and fathers; and to provide income and tax supports for families that would ease the need to maximize market hours while providing incentives for more-equal divisions of labor.

First, paid maternity leave and decent child care would go a long way toward supporting the employment of mothers with young children. Women begin to incur the mommy tax shortly after they have their first child, especially if they're not entitled to paid maternity leave—and most American women are not. All of the Western European nations and many developing countries grant mothers paid maternity leave financed by social insurance funds. Public-maternity-leave schemes have been found to increase mothers' postnatal employment rates, increase the probability that mothers return to the same employer, and lessen the wage penalty associated with time away.

In addition, high-quality, affordable child care enables mothers to work for pay. As with leave, Americans get incredibly little child-care support from government. In the United States, about 5 percent of children under age three are in publicly provided or financed child care, compared with one-quarter in France, one-third in Belgium and Sweden, and fully half in Denmark. Not surprisingly, in all of those countries, married mothers with young children take home larger shares of parental earnings than do American mothers.

Paternity Leave

Second, paid family leave for fathers, especially if designed with incentives so that fathers actually use the leave, creates a way for men to take off time from employment, temporarily, to provide care at home. Fathers in several European countries are entitled to paternity leave immediately following a birth or adoption and, more consequentially, to paid-parental-leave benefits that can be used throughout the early years of their children's lives. Furthermore, policy makers in Europe have learned that parental-leave benefits that can't be transferred to female partners and that include high wage-replacement rates encourage fathers to take the leave to which they're entitled.

In addition, several European governments are running public-education campaigns that urge men to do more at home, either via family leave or more broadly. While the jury is still out on their effectiveness, even the Swiss government is going this route; an ongoing campaign in Switzerland—"Fair Play at Home"—is aimed at "nudging married men" to share the work at home. Despite all the lip service conservatives pay to the value of marriage, American social policy does almost nothing to encourage fathers in intact families to contribute more at home.

Third, Americans log the longest employment hours in the world. As University of Pennsylvania sociologist Jerry Jacobs observes, long hours on the job and gender equality work at cross-purposes; that is especially true in labor markets that lack options for high-quality, reduced-hour employment. Government policies aimed at shortening standard working time—either directly or via incentives placed on employers—could go a long way toward enabling men to spend more time at home. Several of the European welfare states provide models for working-time regulations designed explicitly to support gender-egalitarian families. Working-time policies (such as maximum hours) can shorten overall hours—a number of countries are aiming to set a new standard of 37.5 hours per week—and "right to time off" policies guarantee parents the right to work part-time while their children are young. (The United States neither limits total hours nor provides rights to time off.) . . .

Finally, income supports and tax reforms would help. Some form of universal child benefit, via transfers or refundable tax credits, could replace some or all of the earnings that couples might sacrifice if husbands lessen their time in employment and wives' increases don't make up the difference. For low-income couples, in particular, cash benefits could relax the necessity to maximize (his) hours in the labor market, no matter how high the personal cost. (Among married couples, average gender differences in employment hours are approximately the same at every point on the income spectrum.) Compared with nearly every country in Europe, the United States spends very little on public income supports for couples with children, even including the Earned Income Tax Credit. And a shift to purely individual-income taxation would encourage a more equal sharing of employment by couples. Joint taxation increases the de facto marginal tax rate on the first dollar earned by the "secondary earner" and that sets up a disincentive for wives' labor-force participation. Individual-income taxation has been implemented in several countries in Europe; it is a major factor underlying Sweden's high female-employment rate. In contrast, the U.S. tax code imposes the same income-tax burden on one- and two-earner couples. Given that employment has fixed costs, this formula disadvantages two-earner couples. . . .

Feminist Marriage: Political Prospects

The good news is that a policy package that would support gender equality in marriage—expanded child care, paid family leave (especially for fathers), and a shift to individual-income taxation—actually has a lot in it for conservatives. These policies support the employment of women (including low-income women), strengthen fathers' ties to their children, and could raise marriage rates—all elements of the current conservative agenda. The problem is that most conservatives will resist expanding social-policy outlays and granting women the freedom to choose nontraditional roles.

Feminists could hasten public support for gender-egalitarian marriage by clarifying, for conservatives and progressives alike, that feminists do not hate marriage per se and never have. In 1871, Elizabeth Cady Stanton wrote: "Conservatism cries out we are going to destroy the family. Timid reformers answer, the . . . equality of woman will not change it. They are both wrong. It will entirely revolutionize it." Stanton was right. Truly egalitarian marriage will be revolutionary—and when it's achieved, feminists will celebrate.

"Modesty . . . invites and protects the evocation of real love."

A Return to Modesty Would Improve Male/Female Relations

Wendy Shalit

According to Wendy Shalit in the following viewpoint, the sexual revolution in the 1960s destroyed the value society placed on modesty. She contends that many of the problems that occur between men and women, including sexual harassment and date rape, stem from women's loss of modesty and men's loss of respect for women's modesty. Restoring modesty, in Shalit's opinion, would enhance male/female relations by reminding men and women that the human body is precious and should be revered and respected. Shalit is the author of *A Return to Modesty: Discovering the Lost Virtue.*

As you read, consider the following questions:
1. Why did Shalit first become interested in modesty?
2. According to the author, how did early feminists regard modesty?
3. What are three myths about modesty, as stated by Shalit?

Wendy Shalit, speech at Hillsdale College, Hillsdale, Michigan, November 15, 2000. Copyright © 2000 by Wendy Shalit. Reproduced by permission of Hillsdale College.

This afternoon I was reading a magazine for brides in which a woman had submitted the following question: "My fiancé wants us to move in together, but I want to wait until we're married. Am I doing our marriage an injustice?" The editor responded: "Your fiancé should understand why you want to wait to share a home. Maybe you're concerned about losing your identity as an individual. Or maybe you're concerned about space issues."

Space issues? Losing her identity? If this woman cared about those things she wouldn't want to get married in the first place. Her question was a moral one. She wanted to know what would be best for her marriage. And on this—however unbeknownst to the magazine's new-agey editor—the evidence is in: Couples who live together before marriage are much less likely to get married; and if they do marry, they're more likely to get divorced. Yet the vocabulary of modesty has largely dropped from our cultural consciousness; when a woman asks a question that necessarily implicates it, we can only mumble about "space issues."

Bathroom Blues

I first became interested in the subject of modesty for a rather mundane reason—because I didn't like the bathrooms at Williams College. Like many enlightened colleges and universities these days, Williams houses boys next to girls in its dormitories and then has the students vote by floor on whether their common bathrooms should be coed. It's all very democratic, but the votes always seem to go in the coed direction because no one wants to be thought a prude. When I objected, I was told by my fellow students that I "must not be comfortable with [my] body." Frankly, I didn't get that, because I was fine with my body; it was their bodies in such close proximity to mine that I wasn't thrilled about.

I ended up writing about this experience in *Commentary* as a kind of therapeutic exercise. But when my article was reprinted in *Reader's Digest*, a weird thing happened: I got piles of letters from kids who said, "I thought I was the only one who couldn't stand these bathrooms." How could so many people feel they were the "only ones" who believed in privacy and modesty? It was troubling that they were afraid to speak up. When and why, I wondered, did modesty become such a taboo?

At Yale in 1997, a few years after my own coed bathroom protest, five Orthodox Jewish students petitioned the administration for permission to live off-campus instead of in coed dorms. In denying them, a dean with the Dickensian name of Brodhead explained that "Yale has its own rules and requirements, which we insist on because they embody our values and beliefs." Yale has no core curriculum, of course, but these coed bathrooms, according to Dean Brodhead, embody its beliefs. I would submit that as a result of this kind of "liberationist" ideology, we today have less, not more freedom, than in the pre-1960s era when modesty was upheld as a virtue. In this regard it's important to recall that when colleges had separate dorms for men and women, and all the visitation rules that went with them, it was also possible for kids to circumvent those rules. It was possible, for instance—now, I'm not advocating this—for students to sneak into each others' dorms and act immodestly. But in the new culture of "liberation," a student can't sneak into the dorms and be modest, or, more accurately, she can't sneak out. There is no "right of exit" in today's immodest society. If you don't participate, you're a weirdo. Hence students are not really free to develop their best selves, to act in accordance with their hopes.

Modesty's Loss, Social Pathology's Gain

Many of the problems we hear about today—sexual harassment, date rape, young women who suffer from eating disorders and report feeling a lack of control over their bodies—are all connected, I believe, to our culture's attack on modesty. Listen, first, to the words we use to describe intimacy: what once was called "making love," and then "having sex," is now "hooking up"—like airplanes refueling in flight. In this context I was interested to learn, while researching for my book, that the early feminists actually praised modesty as ennobling to society. Here I'm not just talking about the temperance-movement feminists, who said, "Lips that touch liquor shall never touch mine." I'm talking about more recent feminists like Simone de Beauvoir, who warned in her book, *The Second Sex*, that if society trivializes modesty, violence against women would result. And she was right. Since the 1960s, when our cultural arbiters deemed this age-old virtue a "hang-up," men have grown to expect women to be casual about sex, and women for their part don't feel they have the right to say "no." This has brought us all more misery than joy. On MTV I have seen a 27-year-old woman say she was "sort of glad" that she had herpes, because now she has "an excuse to say 'no' to sex." For her, disease had replaced modesty as the justification for exercising free choice.

The Right to Modesty

Just as our great-grandmothers questioned the validity of a system which denied them their rights as citizens of a free country, we must question the validity of a culture which denies us our most basic rights as females. We have a right to our modesty. It's a natural, healthy impulse to refrain from certain activities and behaviors, yet our society has conditioned whole generations of young girls to reject that impulse. The result is nothing more than free and easy sex for men and heartache for women. We have a right to become full-time wives and mothers and in fact we should be encouraged to do so.

Bronwen McShea, *Harvard Salient*, March 3, 1999.

In 1948 there was a song called "Baby It's Cold Outside" by Frank Loesser, in which a boyfriend wants his girlfriend to sleep over. His argument is simple but compelling: Baby it's cold outside, and if she doesn't sleep over, she could catch pneumonia and die, and that would cause him "lifelong sorrow." In response, the girl offers several counter-arguments: "My father will be waiting at the door, there's bound to be talk tomorrow," etc. It's a very cute song. And while post-modern intellectuals at progressive institutions like Yale would no doubt say this song proves how oppressed women were in 1948, I would argue that today's culture—in which fathers can't be counted on to be waiting at the door—is far creepier.

The counterpoint to "Baby It's Cold Outside" is a story I read in a women's magazine, written by an ex-boyfriend of an 18-year-old girl whose father had decided that she was too old to be a virgin. After commiserating with the boyfriend, this father drove the pair to a hotel (he didn't trust the boyfriend with his car), where the girl became hysterical and the scheme fell apart. This article was called "My Ex-Girlfriend's Father: What a Man!" And although the story isn't typical, it is quite common these days for parents to rent hotel rooms for their kids on prom nights, which is essentially the same principle. So the father in "Baby It's Cold Outside" waiting at the door, and the older culture that supported modesty, actually made women stronger. It gave them the right to say 'no' until they met someone they wanted to marry. Today's culture of "liberation" gives women no ground on which to stand. And an immodest culture weakens men, too we are all at the mercy of other people's judgment of us as sexual objects (witness the revolution in plastic surgery for men), which is not only tiring but also dishonest because we can't be ourselves.

When I talk to college students, invariably one will say, "Well, if you want to be modest, be modest. If you want to be promiscuous, be promiscuous. We all have a choice, and that's the wonderful thing about this society." But the culture, I tell them, can't be neutral. Nor is it subtle in its influence on behavior. In fact, culture works more like a Sherman tank. In the end, if it's not going to value modesty, it will value promiscuity and adultery, and all our lives and marriages will suffer as a result.

Four Myths Exposed

A first step toward reviving respect for modesty in our culture is to strike at the myths that undermine it. Let me touch on four of these.

The first myth is that modesty is Victorian. But what about the [biblical] story of Rebecca and Isaac? When Rebecca sees Isaac and covers herself, it is not because she is trying to be Victorian. Her modesty was the key to what would bring them together and develop a profound intimacy. When we cover up what is external or superficial—what we all share in common—we send a message that what is most important are our singular hearts and minds. This separates us from the animals, and always did, long before the Victorian era.

The second myth about modesty is that it's synonymous with prudery. This was the point of the dreadful movie *Pleasantville*, the premise of which was that nobody in the 1950s had fun or experienced love. It begins in black and white and turns to color only when the kids enlighten their parents about sex. This of course makes no sense on its face: if the parents didn't know how to do it, then how did all these kids get there in the first place? But it reflects a common conceit of baby boomers that passion, love and happiness were nonexistent until modesty was overcome in the 1960s. In truth, modesty is nearly the opposite of prudery. Paradoxically, prudish people have more in common with the promiscuous. The prudish and the promiscuous share a disposition against allowing themselves to be moved by others, or to fall in love. Modesty, on the other hand, invites and protects the evocation of real love. It is erotic, not neurotic.

To illustrate this point, I like to compare photographs taken at Coney Island almost a century ago with photographs from nude beaches in the 1970s. At Coney Island, the beachgoers are completely covered up, but the men and women are stealing glances at one another and seem to be having a great time. On the nude beaches, in contrast, men and women hardly look at each other—rather, they look at the sky. They appear completely bored. That's what those who came after the '60s discovered about this string of dreary hookups: without anything left to the imagination, sex becomes boring.

Rooted in Nature

The third myth is that modesty isn't natural. This myth has a long intellectual history, going back at least to [philosopher] David Hume, who argued that society invented modesty so that men could be sure that children were their own. As [philosopher Jean-Jacques] Rousseau pointed out, this argument that modesty is a social construct suggests that it is possible to get rid of modesty altogether. Today we try to do just that, and it is widely assumed that we are succeeding. But are we?

In arguing that Hume was wrong and that modesty is rooted in nature, a recently discovered hormone called oxytocin comes to mind. This hormone creates a bonding response when a mother is nursing her child, but is also released during intimacy. Here is physical evidence that women become emotionally bonded to their sexual partners even if they only intend a more casual encounter. Modesty protected this natural emotional vulnerability; it made women strong. But we don't really need to resort to physiology to see the naturalness of modesty. We can observe it on any windy day when women wearing slit skirts hobble about comically to avoid showing their legs—the very legs those fashionable skirts are designed to reveal. Despite trying to keep up with the fashions, these women have a natural instinct for modesty.

The fourth and final myth I want to touch on is that modesty is solely a concern for women. We are where we are today only in part because the feminine ideal has changed. The masculine ideal has followed suit. It was once looked on as manly to be faithful to one woman for life, and to be protective toward all women. Sadly, this is no longer the case, even among many men to whom modest women might otherwise look as kindred spirits. Modern feminists are wrong to expect men to be gentlemen when they themselves are not ladies, but men who value "scoring" and then lament that there are no modest women around anymore—well, they are just as bad. And of course, a woman can be modestly dressed and still be harassed on the street. So the reality is that a lot depends on male respect for modesty. It is characteristic of modern society that everyone wants the other guy to be nice to him without having to change his own behavior, whether it's the feminists blaming the men, the men blaming the feminists, or young people blaming their role models. But that is an infantile posture.

Restoring a Modest Society

Jews read a portion of the Torah each week, and in this week's portion there is a story that shows us beautifully, I think, how what we value in women and men are inextricably linked. Abraham is visited by three men, really three angels, and he is providing them with his usual hospitality, when they ask him suddenly, "Where is Sarah your wife?" And he replies, famously, "Behold! In the tent!" Commentators ask, why in the world are the angels asking where Sarah is? They know she is in the tent. They are, after all, angels. And one answer is, to remind Abraham of where she is, in order to increase his love for her. This is very interesting, because in Judaism the most important work takes place, so to speak, "in the tent"— keeping kosher, keeping the Sabbath, keeping the laws of marital purity. Torah is only passed on to the next generation because of what the woman is doing in the home. Yet it is not enough for there to be a Sarah who is in the tent; it is also necessary that there be an Abraham who appreciates her. So I think the lesson is clear if we want to reconstruct a more modest, humane society, we have to start with ourselves.

I don't think it's an accident that the most meaningful explication of modesty comes from the Bible. I was fascinated in my research to discover how many secular women are returning to modesty because they found, simply as a practical matter, that immodesty wasn't working for them. In short, they weren't successful finding the right men. For me this prompts an essentially religious question: Why were we created in this way? Why can't we become happy by imitating the animals? In the sixth chapter of Isaiah we read that the fiery angels surrounding the throne of God have six wings. One set is for covering the face, another for covering the legs, and only the third is for flying. Four of the six wings, then, are for modesty's sake. This beautiful image suggests that the more precious something is, the more it must conceal and protect itself. The message of our dominant culture today, I'm afraid, is that we're not precious, that we weren't created in the divine image. I'm saying to the contrary that we were, and that as such we deserve modesty.

"If modern society suddenly adopted calling cards and modesty pieces, it would not enjoy an instant moral restoration."

Arguments for a Return to Modesty Are Flawed

Jonah Goldberg

In the following viewpoint Jonah Goldberg criticizes Wendy Shalit's book *A Return to Modesty: Discovering the Lost Virtue*. He contends that Shalit advocates old-fashioned customs, such as arranged marriages and calling cards, because they preserved a woman's modesty and contributed to respectful relations between men and women. In Goldberg's opinion, Shalit's arguments are flawed because due to many of the antiquated customs she endorses, women were owned and controlled by men. This patriarchal control, according to Goldberg, often led to the rape and abuse of women. Thus, modesty and other old-fashioned customs, Goldberg maintains, do not improve relations between men and women. Goldberg is a contributing editor and online columnist for the *National Review*.

As you read, consider the following questions:

1. According to Goldberg, what does Shalit have in common with other feminists?
2. As quoted by the author, why does Shalit want to return to the Victorian era?
3. Why were dating rituals established, as stated by Goldberg?

Jonah Goldberg, "Conservatism Without History," *Reason*, vol. 31, May 1999, p. 64. Copyright © 1999 by the Reason Foundation, 3415 S. Sepulveda Blvd., Suite 400, Los Angeles, CA 90034. www.reason.com. Reproduced with permission.

[T]he 1990s were] a very strange decade for the women's movement. It began with feminists lionizing the fictional Murphy Brown for having a baby without a husband. Now the equally fictional Ally McBeal has inspired *Time* to ask "Is Feminism Dead?" because she likes men, thinks sex is both fun and a big deal, and really wants to be married before she's a mother. When the '90s were young, [writer] Katie Roiphe made it big pointing out that radical feminists had largely concocted the date rape crisis. More recently, she wrote that sleeping with the boss is a winning strategy for can-do women. [Feminist] Naomi Wolfe has championed promiscuity but retreated somewhat on abortion; [feminist] Camille Paglia has made a cottage industry out of celebrating kinky sex, pornography, and, most of all, herself.

And then, of course, there is the president's contribution. 1991 seems like an alien planet now, with feminists flaying an unmarried Clarence Thomas for asking an employee for a date. Eight years later, it's no big deal for the married commander-in-chief to have sex with an intern. Indeed, according to some feminist writers such as Jane Smiley writing in *The New Yorker*, [Bill] Clinton's behavior simply reflected a human "desire to make a connection with another person." On *Meet the Press* then-Sen. Carol Mosely Braun (D-Ill.), a woman swept into office by the backlash against Clarence Thomas, defended the president's behavior by observing, "Thirty years ago women weren't even allowed to be White House interns."

The only conclusion one can draw from all this is that the market for feminist commentary is as open as the definition of feminism itself.

The Personal Is Political

Enter Wendy Shalit, author of *A Return to Modesty: Discovering the Lost Virtue*. Shalit has a lot in common with the decade's other feminist and anti-feminist newcomers. She's young. She's smart. And she believes in perhaps the only axiom to be passed down intact from the previous generation: "The personal is political."

Therein lies the twist. Rather than claim, like some of her peers, that her catalog of one-night stands, unrequited lust, dysfunctional relationships, and sexual misadventures gives her the authority to dictate morality to others, Shalit asserts the opposite. Her moral stature derives from the fact that she doesn't put out.

A very recent graduate of Williams College, Shalit made her breakthrough with an article in *Commentary* about her horror at her dorm's introduction of coed bathrooms. From there, she garnered a reputation as a neoconservative wunderkind, with a billet at the *City Journal* in New York City. *A Return to Modesty*, her first book, represents the first major attempt to provide an intellectual framework for "True Love Waits" and the rest of the pro-virginity movement. Shalit offers a sustained defense of chastity, extolling the virtues of 19th- (if not seventh-) century social and sexual norms. Sex before marriage is an abomination, she declares. Even heavy petting is distasteful.

Recently, *The New York Observer* asked her if all this sounded a bit "neo-Victorian." She responded, "No, just Victorian." And why does Shalit want to return to the Victorian era? Because, she told the *Observer*, "I want to make things better."

That may be cute and provocative, but intellectually it is an absolute surrender to nostalgia. If Shalit had argued for the "neo," she might have had me. But I can no more live in Victorian England than I can join Star Fleet Academy.

Inadequate Remedies

To be fair, if one holds Shalit's view of the world, things certainly couldn't get any worse, and 1850s England would be a welcome cultural harbor. Shalit may be the only writer around who believes both the sky-is-falling feminists and the we're-all-going-to-hell social conservatives. The left and the right have diagnosed different symptoms of the same social affliction, she argues. It's the remedies they've prescribed that are inadequate: "Girls who can't say no, anorexic girls, girls who are mutilating their bodies, girls who are stalked or raped, many who never see their fathers—and from the Left, the advice we get is, 'Whatever you do, don't be romantic,' and from the Right, 'Whatever you do, don't become a feminist.'"

It's left to Shalit to offer the magic elixir, the cure for what ails everyone: modesty. "It is no accident that harassment, stalking, and rape all increased when we decided to let everything hang out," she writes. "A society that has declared war on embarrassment is one that is hostile to women."

One could easily quibble here. One might dispute the way Shalit characterizes each faction's advice to young women, or point out that the data on stalking and self-mutilation are of a recent and unreliable vintage. But quibbles do not get to the heart of the problem with this book: For a conservative, Shalit has remarkably little appreciation for history. She may pine for an age of long skirts, quaint courtship rituals, modesty pieces, and Talmudic injunctions against touching, along with every other cultural barrier that ever has been erected between the sexes. But for all her love of the rituals of the past, she pays no homage to the historical contexts that created them.

For example: Shalit writes nostalgically about calling cards and their demise. She points out, correctly, that for most of Western history, people didn't want unmarried men and women to be alone together, even during courtship. Calling cards expedited the courting process without rocking the boat too much. A gentleman in pursuit of a young lady would drop off a card at her home to request a personal visit. If the woman declined the invitation, both she and her suitor would be saved face-to-face embarrassment.

Shalit loves this idea, and she doesn't seem to think there's any reason why we can't have it back. It has not occurred to her, apparently, that people used calling cards before we had this neat invention called the "telephone."

Accepting Romantic Choice

Calling cards were a small part of an ongoing social compromise with the rising middle class's increasing willingness to accept romantic choice. Arranged marriages were giving way to the insight that people should be able to select their spouse, or at least have some say in the decision. So elaborate dating rituals emerged, offering ways to pay tribute to tradition while still affording greater liberty in choosing a partner. We still use many of these rituals today, and some of the old traditions are gaining new strength. But Shalit seems unconcerned with all of this. Indeed, she likes arranged marriages too.

And she likes Richard Brathwait's *The English Gentleman* and *The English Gentlewoman*, dated 1630 and 1631 respectively. (According to Brathwait, "bashfull modesty" was a woman's ticket to salvation: "Modesty must be your guide, vertuous thoughts your guard, so shall heaven be your goale.") From Shalit's rendering, you might think Brathwait's interesting treatises are travel brochures for a cultural Shangri-la, a utopia to which we can easily return by clicking our heels or reading her book. The reality, of course, is that in the 1630s birth control was almost non-existent and reproduction mysterious. Women were often chattel; marriages were often arranged.

Enslaved Virtue

Wendy Shalit, at the tender age of 23, made the case for the virgin bride in *A Return to Modesty*. The book was essentially a retread of the old chestnut: "Why buy the cow when you can get the milk for free?" Shalit pointed approvingly to the way women are treated in Islamic and Orthodox Jewish cultures in which rules against the mingling of the sexes before marriage is strictly enforced.

Funny, when I look at a burka-clad woman, the beneficial protection of her virtue isn't the first thing that springs to mind.

Robyn E. Blumner, *St. Petersburg Times*, April 21, 2002.

Shalit seems to think that if she can only explain why the olden days were better than today—if only we could understand the things she does—we could transform society overnight. But ideas neither last in a vacuum nor spring forth ex nihilo. Of course some values have eroded in the last century. But the cause of those changes cannot solely be found in the intellectual realm. The automobile probably did more to destabilize traditional values than [philosopher Friedrich] Nietzsche did. One can argue with Nietzsche. But who, besides [vice president] Al Gore, will argue with the car?

Shalit ignores the essential insight of modern conservatives, from [philosopher Edmund] Burke to [statesman Benjamin] Disraeli: Ancient wisdom is a vital guide for reform, not a replacement for it. Human nature, to borrow [economic theorist] Glenn Loury's phrase, has no history. But institutions must have a history; if they do not change with the times, they die. If modern society suddenly adopted calling cards and modesty pieces, it would not enjoy an instant moral restoration. It would be hobbled with kitsch.

Poor Research

This might have been prevented if Shalit had researched her book more diligently. [Conservative pundit] William F. Buckley has argued that the neoconservatives' great contribution to the American right was sociology: Where older conservatives had contented themselves with philosophical arguments, the neocons deployed data. But the younger generation of neocons seems to have given up on rigor. Shalit cites perhaps a thousand women's magazines and maybe five actual studies. Letters to *Marie Clare* may be interesting as anecdotes or as culture chaff, but intellectually they have the nutritional value of a styrofoam cup. She would have been better off exploring, say, sociobiology, a field rich in data that have a great deal to say about modesty.

She also might have been more wary of inconsistencies. In her introduction, she writes sweetly about the idea of fathers giving away their daughters at weddings: "What is really so terrible about 'belonging' to someone who loves you?" Thirty-five pages later she attacks a notorious 1976 British House of Lords case, *Regina v. Morgan*, as a symptom of the decline of modesty. There is a contradiction here, and she misses it.

Regina is a staple feminist anecdote. One evening a man got drunk with three of his buddies. He told them that his wife was really kinky and that she would love it if they each had their way with her. Intrigued, the men went back to his house, where they proceeded to take turns raping his wife. The Lords ruled that the men weren't really guilty of rape because they believed there was implied consent.

Shalit, rightly horrified, believes that old-fashioned notions of modesty would have prevented this episode. (Maybe, maybe not: I'm not convinced that such atrocities did not occur a century ago.) Nevertheless, she sees no tension between extolling a system that says a father can own and then give away a daughter and denouncing the view that once the husband takes possession of the woman he can do as he pleases with her. Paternal ownership and matrimonial ownership are of the same piece—historically, intellectually, theologically. In the Third World nations where these institutions still exist—China, India, Central Asia—fathers regularly sell their daughters. If the daughters are lucky, they're sold to a husband.

A Return to Modesty is engagingly written at times, and Shalit's style will doubtless be most effective where it will do the most good: among young women who fear they are alone in questioning Naomi Wolfe's paean to the "shadow slut." Some of Shalit's critics have derided her for being a prude, but that criticism is unfair. If she had partied like a hooker during fleet week, she would have been accused of hypocrisy and dismissed out of hand.

And, yes, Shalit is very bright. But her book is sophomoric in its overconfident ambition. It would be more persuasive if it were a bit more modest.

"The assault against men must stop."

Ending Male Bashing Would Improve Male/Female Relations

Wendy McElroy

According to Wendy McElroy in the following viewpoint, men are subjected to crude jokes and unfair generalizations that society would consider outrageous if directed at blacks or women. McElroy contends that as a result of male bashing, boys are falling behind in schools and men are neglected by the health care industry. McElroy maintains that most men are decent, hardworking individuals who deserve to be treated with respect. McElroy is the editor of *Liberty for Women* and *Freedom, Feminism, and the State*, and the author of several books, including *XXX: A Woman's Right to Pornography* and *Sexual Correctness: The Gender Feminist Attack on Women.*

As you read, consider the following questions:
1. How does the author define male bashing?
2. What three steps does the author advocate to stop male bashing?
3. In McElroy's opinion, why are men ignored by the media?

Wendy McElroy, "Cut Men: Do They Not Bleed?" www.ifeminists.net, May 13, 2003. Copyright © 2003 by Wendy McElroy. Reproduced by permission.

M ale bashing—the stereotyping of men as brutal, stupid or otherwise objectionable—is commonplace. Our sons, husbands, fathers and men-friends are gleefully slandered because they are male. They are subjected to malicious jokes and attitudes that would be decried if directed at blacks, Hispanics or women. The assault against men must stop. But how?

Damage to Men

The message that being male is somehow seriously wrong and should be controlled has been broadcast for over three decades. That message is now embedded in laws such as affirmative action and in policies such as bias against fathers in family courts. The damage inflicted on the men in our lives is clear.

- As children, boys are falling behind in the public school system, a process that Christina Hoff Sommers [author of *The War Against Boys: How Misguided Feminism Is Harming Our Young Men*] has thoroughly and persistently documented.
- As young adults, male students on American campuses are outnumbered by females by a ratio of four to three, with males receiving only 43 percent of all college degrees.
- In middle age, men are badly slighted by public policies. For example, "women's health" receives far more funding despite the fact that men have higher rates in all but one of the 15 leading causes of death. The May [2003] issue of the *American Journal of Public Health* cites social factors as an important contributing cause.
- In old age, the average man is likely to die five years before the average woman. Only now is this disparity being called "a silent health crisis."

From cradle to grave, men are routinely disadvantaged by social attitudes and the legal system.

The New Victims

A new group of victims has been created: men. But instead of loving them for their victimhood, as our culture is wont to do, men remain the brunt of political rage and accusations.

Greeting Card Misandry

Any man who rapes or commits other violent crimes deserves to be shunned. But he should be reviled by name for specific acts, not for his gender any more than a violent black person should be reviled for his/her race. It is wrong to blame the large majority of decent men for the actions of the indecent few.

Stand by Your Man

There are several steps you can take right now to stand up for the men in your life:

1. Take a personal stand. This is the most important step toward halting the gender war: People should refuse to participate in it. Don't hurl insults at "all men"; if a specific man has wronged you, insult him by name. Don't go along with the male bashing of girlfriends or co-workers. You don't have to become angry—indeed, you should not; instead, calmly disagree or point out that maligning fellow employees is bad for the workplace. If that step is too awkward for you, then at least don't join in. For example, don't laugh at jokes that skewer "all men," including your infant son.

2. Take an economic stand. Boycott companies who use blatantly anti-male commercials to sell their products or services. For example, Progressive Insurance ran a notorious ad in which an angry woman punished her ex through a voodoo doll, including the use of pliers on its genitals. Imagine how

you would react if the genital ripping had been inflicted on a woman. Go to the Web site of such companies and tell them why they will not be receiving your money. And while you are at it, refuse to watch TV shows in which all the male characters are portrayed as buffoons . . . or much worse. Make male bashing uncommercial.

3. Take a political stand. Do not support laws or policies, like Title IX,[1] that disadvantage your son to benefit your daughter, or vice versa. Let your children be judged on their merits as individuals. On the other hand, do support campaigns that make gender inequities in the law more visible. For example, talk about the problem of men who are battered in domestic violence. A November 1998 Department of Justice report states that 834,732 men are victims of physical violence by an intimate and they deserve as much support as battered women.

"I Object"

Small actions on your part are powerful. The columnist John Leo illustrates this by recounting a joke presented by a woman speaker: "A woman needed a brain transplant. Her doctor said two brains were available, a woman's brain for $500 and a man's brain for $5,000. Why the big price difference? Answer: The woman's brain has been used." A man in the audience objected to the joke as male bashing and asked people to substitute "black" or "Jew" for the word "man." Just saying "I object" is powerful.

Carry the word substitution one step farther. When you hear claims with specific gender references, switch the gender and think about the message. For example, you hear that separating a mother from her child is a terrible thing. What about separating a father from his child?

It cannot be overstated: Most men are good, hard-working human beings who love their families and never raise a hand in violence. Because their decency is not sensational, they are ignored by media and politicians who focus instead on men who rape or otherwise give their gender a bad name. A better reaction is to hold the decent men closer to us and value them more.

---

1. Title IX, of the Education Amendments of 1972, governs the equity of treatment and opportunity for girls and boys in school athletics.

> *"The men's and fathers' movement needs to make sure it never sees females as the enemy."*

Ending Woman Bashing Would Improve Male/Female Relations

Glenn Sacks

In the following viewpoint Glenn Sacks argues that some advocates of the men's movement engage in slanderous denunciations of women that resemble the man-bashing men have endured since the feminist movement began in the 1960s. Woman bashers, according to Sacks, believe that all women are to blame for society's problems, that women have succeeded at the expense of men, and that feminism is the cause of all fathers' and men's troubles. Sacks maintains that if gender relations are ever to improve, supporters of the men's movement should work together to end woman bashing. Glenn Sacks is a men's and fathers' issues columnist and a nationally syndicated radio talk show host.

As you read, consider the following questions:

1. According to Sacks, why do woman bashers believe that male-friendly females have dubious motives?
2. How is using personal experience to denigrate women harmful, in the author's opinion?
3. As stated by Sacks, how is the men's movement different from the civil rights movement?

It is said "choose your enemies carefully, for someday you'll resemble them." The men's and fathers' movement is gaining in strength and slowly making progress. However, there is a disturbing fringe element whose woman-bashing very much resembles the vicious man-bashing which men and fathers have endured for the past three decades. It is important that men's and fathers' activists confront this fringe rather than turn a blind eye to it.

Believing All Women Are the Problem

Characteristic #1: The woman-basher believes that all women, or virtually all women, are the problem.

For example, in a recent issue of *Transitions*, the newsletter of the National Coalition of Free Men [NCFM], a front cover cartoon depicts a pretty bride (representing a woman on her wedding day), and then a hideous, multi-headed monster (representing a woman in divorce court, presumably because she has won custody of the children and driven the father out of his children's lives). The caption reads, "This is a female. She will destroy your life in ways you never thought possible." Most NCFM leaders and members immediately recognized the unjustness of the cartoon, and realized that it was, in fact, a perfect mirror of the radical feminist "all men are rapists" position.

Another woman-basher (WB) expressed similar thoughts in a later issue, writing that for men, bad things "will happen if you engage in risky behavior such as having sex, having a child, getting married, or [having] anything resembling a relationship with a woman." The writer cautions that those who dismiss these inevitabilities are "the future victims."

Characteristic #2: WBs believe that men don't ever really oppose woman-bashing or woman-blaming, but oppose it publicly only because they're forced to do so.

After the cover cartoon was published, there was a storm of protest from NCFM members and leaders, and the issue was hotly debated in the pages of *Transitions*. Many WBs, however, assumed that these protests (and the ensuing anti-woman-bashing measures taken by the Board of Directors) were made because we were afraid of our wives' reproach or because we feared offending some by not being politically correct. The idea that most NCFM members and leaders opposed the cartoon out of simple fairness and decency did not seem to occur to them. This is similar to the feminist view that any woman who opposes feminism can't really be against feminism, but is instead the dupe or the captive of evil, reactionary males.

Dubious Motives

Characteristic #3: WBs believe that even those females who have helped us do so out of dubious motives.

When syndicated columnist Kathleen Parker recently launched a misguided attack on Russell Yates,[1] one men's chat-room participant derided Parker as a "Giggling ditz-bunny" who is "another Cathy Young, another Wendy McElroy—one of those women whose image of herself is so pompously filled with patronizing goodwill towards the poor little men that she can't even imagine how sexist and anti-male she sounds."

Another noted that male-friendly female writers like McElroy are simply like the "farmer [who] always fattens up the turkey before Thanksgiving." The farmer is always "meticulously friendly" but has "malevolence in her heart." We are also told that McElroy's ideology is that of "friendly fascist feminism" and that women like this don't bash men because they instead try to "neuter them politely."

An outside observer would never guess that the WBs are speaking of the small minority of writers who have actually made a real effort to discuss men's issues at a time when it hasn't been popular to do so.

At the Expense of Each Other

Characteristic #4: WBs believe that for 30 years women have won at the expense of men and that men can only win now at the expense of women.

As [writer] Warren Farrell says, when only one sex wins, both sexes lose. There is no way that men or women can

---

1. Russell Yates's wife, Andrea Yates, was convicted in 2002 of drowning their five children. She had a history of postpartum depression, and Russell Yates was criticized for continuing to have children with a woman who was clearly unstable and posed a threat to her babies.

move forward from this point unless they move forward together and on an equitable basis.

Characteristic #5: WBs dismiss women's contributions to
our movement because "it's often women who speak up for
us only because Lace Curtain[2] censorship doesn't allow men
to do it."

Lace Curtain censorship is real, and yes, many men have
been silenced, but this doesn't discredit the efforts of those
women who have spoken out. It is important that we don't
mistreat them, as the feminists did to the many men who
helped the cause of women's liberation. Dianna Thompson,
the Executive Director of the American Coalition of Fathers
and Children (ACFC), says:

> I can understand men's frustration. It's unfair that women are
> typically able to talk more about gender issues than men can.
> If I talk about the way current child support guidelines are
> excessive and unfairly burdensome to fathers, people will lis-
> ten. If a man says the same thing, people will look at him and
> say 'He's just trying to get out of paying.' It's not fair and I
> don't like it, but I'm not the one who made these rules.
> Women in the fathers' movement didn't make these rules.

An Impossible Double-Bind

Women who have helped men and fathers often find themselves in an impossible double-bind—they are labeled
traitors by feminist-minded women, and at the same time
are disparaged by WBs. Trudy Schuett, publisher of the
Desert Light Journal, has been denounced by feminists as a
"fathers' rights whore," and [writer] Susan Faludi has implied that pro-father women are Uncle Toms. Kim Gandy,
the president of the National Organization for Women, says
that the relationship between men and women in the fathers'
movement is similar to the way "a man charged with rape
will hire a woman lawyer to represent him."

Conversely, some women in the fathers' movement report
that there are men who contact fathers groups and are dis-
pleased when a woman answers the phone or when a female

2. According to Warren Farrell, the Lace Curtain is "the tendency of most major
institutions to interpret gender issues from only a feminist perspective or from a
combination of feminist and female perspectives."

activist is chosen to help them.

Since some men apparently have forgotten those many women to whom we owe a debt of gratitude, I have begun to compile a list of male-friendly women activists and writers who deserve recognition.

Men Harm Each Other

If men more generally are to find emotionally richer and more satisfying lives, they are going to have to accept that women have never been the main cause of their fears and insecurities. It has been men themselves, in their attempts to preserve privilege through exclusion. Today's male moaners (so threatened by women's search for equality), weekend warriors (still seeking mythic escape from women's clutches), or virile disciplinarians (aiming to toughen up men for competition and survival, while returning women to the kitchens) are merely keeping men in harness to an ideology which has damaged them, while tyrannising women.

Lynne Segal, *Red Pepper*, March 1999.

Characteristic #6: WBs believe that when male-friendly women writers or activists show support for the mainstream feminist view of a gender issue, it is indicative of their bad intentions.

Young, McElroy, and Parker have together tackled a laundry list of men's issues, yet when they've disagreed with men's activists (such as Young and Parker's recent attacks on Russell Yates), some WBs have been quick to accuse them of selling-out or of double-dealing. In reality, when these women have disagreed with men's activists they've sometimes been right. More importantly, disagreement and independence (as well as concern about legitimate women's issues) don't indicate betrayal or malevolence. And while I disagree with Young on the culpability of Russell Yates, her central point—that fathers' activists should not defend fathers simply because they are fathers—is a valid one.

Using Personal Experience

Characteristic #7: WBs use personal experience (having children stolen in a divorce, being the victim of false accusations or of domestic violence, etc.) to justify anti-female bigotry.

This is a dangerous practice, because it parallels the despicable way feminists have used victimhood to justify man-hate. One need only to look at the hate-filled feminist head case Andrea Dworkin, reputedly the victim of sexual abuse, to see where this leads. Pain and victimization need to be channeled into reasonable and dedicated political action, not woman-bashing.

A healthy response to victimization is to emulate McElroy, a former victim of severe domestic violence. Rather than turning her personal victimization into anti-male bigotry, she has used it to gain insight into the lives of all victims of domestic violence, male and female.

Blaming Feminism

Characteristic #8: WBs believe that feminism has caused all of men's and fathers' current problems.

WBs blame feminism but ignore an equally destructive force—men's chivalrous tendency to blame men first and women last. It is this attitude which has created what Farrell calls "the machinery of male protection," whose victims are almost always male.

For example, in a discussion of the Texas District Attorney who is considering filing charges against Russell Yates "because of all the e-mails she received" a WB wrote, "Who do you think sent those mails? Women."

I can say from my experiences defending Russell Yates in the *Houston Chronicle* and on radio talk show programs throughout the Southwest that this is a misguided assumption. The most vociferous attacks on Russell (and on me) came not from women, but from men, most of whom have deeply imbided the "always blame the man" ethic of our time. Russell ought to hope for an all-female jury.

Characteristic #9: WBs believe that women aren't worth the trouble.

One WB recently wrote about "a tale I've heard from a number of friends. F—king women in the feminist era is so dangerous that it's not worth the effort, and, anyway, most women are so damned lousy in bed that they aren't worth the trouble." This writer could perhaps find a soulmate in feminist bigot Germaine Greer, who recently said, "God knows how many women already have no use for their men, who are all too often idle and incompetent both as wage-earners and around the house, uninterested in the children and hopeless in bed."

The Radical Model

Characteristic #10: The WBs believe that their "radical" rhetoric and posture helps the men's movement achieve its goals, just as the radicalism of Malcolm X helped Martin Luther King achieve his moderate civil rights goals.

Some WBs justify or even celebrate woman-bashing by referring to the Civil Rights Movement model, whereby white racists knew that if they didn't give the moderate King what he wanted, they'd have to deal with the radical Malcolm.

Setting aside the fact that the above assumptions about King and Malcolm aren't actually historically accurate, there is one fatal flaw with this model. At the time of the Civil Rights movement, most Americans acknowledged that blacks had been mistreated and oppressed. Thus, while Malcolm X could be criticized for his radical views, nobody could deny that the source of his rage was legitimate.

WBs do not, and in many ways should not, enjoy the same legitimacy. Men, as a whole, are still often viewed as oppressors or at least as advantaged. In practical terms, woman-bashing from our quarter often doesn't sound like the noble defiance of the oppressed, but instead like the unjust rage of the "privileged" whose privileges are under attack. Thus woman-bashing marginalizes and delegitimizes all wings of our movement.

The Frustration of Men

To be fair to the WBs, with a few exceptions, their woman-bashing is not the product of genuine misogyny, but is instead reflective of the frustration of a generation of men who have grown up in a relentlessly misandrist popular culture, and who have had almost no forum within which to oppose it. It is also true that over the past three decades we have become so unaccustomed to hearing criticism of women, that legitimate criticism is often labeled "woman-bashing" or "misogyny." But there's an important difference between criticizing certain female behaviors or demanding fairness from women, and the "all women are out to destroy men" attitude of some WBs.

Besides being unjust, woman-bashing could be disastrous for our movement. After 30 years of being on the receiving end of gender abuse, the time is ripe for gender reconciliation and a serious attempt to address men's concerns. The injustices committed against men (particularly fathers) by our courts and our media are so outrageous that most people will support us if we can get the truth out to them. Even many feminist dissidents are tired of man-bashing and victimology, and have rejected anti-male feminism. The special courage—the male courage—of the heroes of [the terrorist attacks on September 11, 2001] has helped remind us of the many unique and critical contributions that men make to our society. We will change society, as long as we are reasonable and fair.

Late in his life Malcolm X said, "the enemy is not whites. The enemy is racism." The men's and fathers' movement needs to make sure it never sees females as the enemy, but only misandry—whether from females or from males. If not, we'll become like the bigoted feminists that this movement was formed to oppose.

Periodical Bibliography

The following articles have been selected to supplement the diverse views presented in this chapter.

John Derbyshire   "It's a Woman's World: The Phasing Out of Men," *National Review*, August 28, 2001.

Andrew Hacker   "How the B.A. Gap Widens the Chasm Between Men and Women," *Chronicle of Higher Education*, June 20, 2003.

Mary E. Hunt   "Battling Patriarchy Within," *Other Side*, September 2000.

Musimbi Kanyoro   "Sitting Down Together," *Other Side*, May/June 1998.

Amy Kass and   "Proposing Courtship," *First Things*, October
Leon Kass   1999.

Linda C. McClain   "Back to Marriage or Servitude?" *Newsday*, April 13, 2003.

Geraldine Murray   "You Won't Find Me on the Chastity Bandwagon," *Sunday Herald*, April 11, 1999.

Amber Pawlik   "Gender Healing: Seeing Bees, Not the Swarm," www.mensnewsdaily.com, September 28, 2003.

Donna L. Sollie   "Beyond Mars and Venus," *National Forum*, Summer 2000.

Anita Taylor   "Men and Women Communicating: Who's from Mars?" *Vital Speeches of the Day*, February 15, 1999.

Agnieszka Tennant   "Nuptial Agreements: Two Models of Marriage Claim Biblical Warrant and Vie for Evangelicals' Allegiance. Advocates of Both Claim Good Results, but Do We Have to Choose?" *Christianity Today*, March 11, 2002.

Cathy Young   "Sex and Sensibility," *Reason*, March 1999.

For Further Discussion

Chapter 1

1. Geoffrey Norman uses his personal observations of girls and boys to support his argument that biological differences establish gender roles. Michael S. Kimmel uses evidence collected by anthropologist Margaret Mead to argue that cultural differences establish gender roles. Whose use of evidence do you think is most persuasive and why?

2. Anne Fausto-Sterling maintains that many people are born with both male and female characteristics, which supports her claim that society should embrace the idea of multiple genders. Leonard Sax disputes Sterling's claims and asserts that there are only two genders, male and female. Think about the possible reasons for each author's different perspective. Why might one person be willing to entertain the idea of multiple genders while another person would argue vociferously for only two genders? Consider social, political, and personal factors while constructing your answer.

Chapter 2

1. Resa LaRue Kirkland argues that feminism has hurt women because it encourages them to enter the workforce, an act which has stripped them of their natural tenderness, the very quality for which men respect them. Katha Pollitt contends that feminism has benefited women by providing them with more opportunities, and she claims that it is wrong to blame feminism for the problems many modern women experience. Do you think tenderness is an inherent female quality? In your opinion, does work outside the home naturally reduce an individual's tenderness? And finally, if some men have lost respect for women because they are less tender as a result of working, should women give up work in order to regain that respect? Cite from the viewpoints while composing your answer. Pay special attention to the way Kirkland defines tenderness.

2. Danielle Crittenden and Jennifer L. Pozner paint very different portraits of men. Examine the way each author depicts men in relation to women. With whose portrait do you most agree? Explain, citing from the texts and drawing on your own experience.

3. Both Sibyl Neimann and Reed Karaim draw heavily from their own personal experiences to draw conclusions about the advisability of mothers staying at home rather than working outside

the home. Whose use of personal experience do you find more persuasive? Explain.

Chapter 3

1. After reading the viewpoints in this chapter, how do you think men's roles have changed in recent years? Do you think those changes have been largely positive or negative? Explain your answers.

2. David Thomas uses personal anecdotes to bolster his argument that fathers are important. Louise B. Silverstein and Carl F. Auerbach cite various studies to support their claim that children do not need fathers. Which argument do you believe is better supported and why?

Chapter 4

1. Steven E. Rhoads asserts that marriages where the husband has the dominant role are more likely to thrive, whereas Janet C. Gornick argues in favor of marriages where the spouses are equally powerful. Based on your readings of the viewpoints and personal observations, which argument do you find more viable? Explain your answer.

2. Wendy Shalit refutes what she considers four myths about modesty. Which, if any, of her assertions do you find most convincing? Which, if any, do you find weak? Explain.

3. A woman, Wendy McElroy, decries male bashing, while Glenn Sacks, a man, is critical of members of the men's movement who slander women. Do you think that their arguments are more effective because they speak in support of the opposite gender? Why or why not?

Organizations to Contact

The editors have compiled the following list of organizations concerned with the issues debated in this book. The descriptions are derived from materials provided by the organizations. All have publications or information available for interested readers. The list was compiled on the date of publication of the present volume; the information provided here may change. Be aware that many organizations take several weeks or longer to respond to inquiries, so allow as much time as possible.

Center for the American Woman and Politics (CAWP)
Eagleton Institute of Politics
Rutgers University, New Brunswick, NJ 08901
(732) 932-9384 • fax: (732) 932-0014
e-mail: gmm@rci.rutgers.edu • Web site: www.rci.rutgers.edu/~cawp
CAWP is a think tank and resource center dedicated to the advancement of women in public leadership. It offers public leadership programs for women, research on the importance of electing women to all levels of government, and current information on the women's political movement. Many of its published materials, including *Political Women Tell What It Takes* and *Women Make a Difference*, are available through its Web site.

Center for the Study of Popular Culture (CSPC)
9911 W. Pico Blvd., Suite 1290, Los Angeles, CA 90035
(310) 843-3699 • fax: (310) 843-3692
e-mail: info@cspc.org • Web site: www.cspc.org
CSPC is a conservative educational and legal-assistance organization addressing such topics as political correctness, feminism, and discrimination. The Individual Rights Foundation, the legal arm of the center, is devoted to establishing gender-neutral standards in public life. The center publishes books, pamphlets, and the magazine *FrontPage*.

Eagle Forum
PO Box 618, Alton, IL 62002
(618) 462-5415 • fax: (618) 462-8909
e-mail: eagle@eagleforum.org • Web site: www.eagleforum.org
Eagle Forum is an educational and political organization that advocates traditional family values. To expose what it perceives as radical feminism's goal to break up the family, the forum examines and disseminates its position on issues such as women in combat, family leave, child care, tax credits for families with children, and

"outcome-based" education. The organization offers several books and publishes the monthly newsletter *The Phyllis Schlafly Report*.

Families and Work Institute (FWI)
267 Fifth Ave., 2nd Fl., New York, NY 10006
(212) 465-2044 • fax: (212) 465-8637
e-mail: publications@familiesandwork.org
Web site: www.familiesandwork.org

The Families and Work Institute is a nonprofit organization that addresses the changing nature of work and family life. It is committed to finding research-based strategies that foster mutually supportive connections among workplaces, families, and communities. More than forty research reports are available for sale from the institute, including *The 1997 National Study of the Changing Workforce, Ahead of the Curve: Why America's Leading Employers are Addressing the Needs of New and Expectant Parents*, and *Working Fathers: New Strategies for Balancing Work and Family*.

The Howard Center
934 N. Main St., Rockford, IL 61103
(815) 964-5819 • fax: (815) 965-1826
e-mail: howard@profam.org • Web site: www.profam.org

The Howard Center works to return America to Judeo-Christian values and supports traditional families and gender roles for men and women. It studies the evolution of the family and the effects of divorce on society. The center offers three monthly publications, *The Family in America, The Religion & Society Report*, and *New Research*.

Independent Women's Forum (IWF)
1726 M St. NW, Suite 1001, Washington, DC 20036
(202) 419-1820
e-mail: info@iwf.org • Web site: www.iwf.org

The Independent Women's Forum is a nonprofit, nonpartisan organization founded by women to foster public education and debate about legal, social, and economic policies affecting women and families. The IWF is committed to policies that promote individual responsibility, limited government, and economic opportunity. It publishes the *Women's Quarterly* journal.

Men's Defense Association
17854 Lyons St., Forest Lake, MN 55025
fax: (651) 464-7887
e-mail: info@mensdefense.org • Web site: www.mensdefense.org

The association promotes equal rights for men and gathers research, compiles statistics, and offers an attorney referral service for male victims of sex discrimination. It publishes the newsmagazine the *Liberator* and the pamphlet *The Men's Manifesto.*

National Center for Fathering

PO Box 413888, Kansas City, MO 64141-3888
(913) 384-4661 • fax: (913) 384-4665
e-mail: dads@fathers.com • Web site: www.fathers.com

The National Center for Fathering is a nonprofit research and education organization that seeks to champion the role of responsible fatherhood by inspiring and equipping men to be more engaged in the lives of children. The center is a resource for men seeking to strengthen their fathering skills. It publishes a wide variety of books about fathering and the quarterly newsletter *Today's Father.*

National Coalition of Free Men (NCFM)

PO Box 582023, Minneapolis, MN 55458
(516) 482-6378
e-mail: ncfm@ncfm.org • Web site: www.ncfm.org

The coalition is a nonprofit educational organization whose mission is to examine men's lives, with particular emphasis on how sex discrimination affects men. In order to raise public consciousness about little-known topics dealing with the male experience, the coalition conducts research, sponsors educational programs, and provides speakers. Its newsletter, *Transitions: Journal of Men's Perspectives*, is published bimonthly and offers statistics, book reviews, movie reviews, and events affecting men.

National Men's Resource Center

PO Box 800, San Anselmo, CA 94979
e-mail: help@menstuff.org • Web site: www.menstuff.org

The National Men's Resource Center is an online nonprofit educational organization dedicated to fostering positive change in male roles and relationships. It offers resources covering all six major segments of the men's movement (men's rights, mythopoetic, profeminist, recovery, reevaluation counseling, and religious) with information on over one hundred men's issues. Its Web site contains information, resources, a calendar of men's events, and an extensive list of publications, including *Silent Sons: A Book for and About Men* and *Proving Manhood: Reflections on Men and Sexism.*

National Organization for Women (NOW)

733 15th St. NW, 2nd Fl., Washington, DC 20005
(202) 628-8669 • fax: (202) 785-8576
e-mail: now@now.org • Web site: www.now.org

The National Organization for Women is a grassroots lobbying organization with over five hundred chapters nationwide. Through education, protests, and litigation, it supports equal rights for women, equal pay for women workers, and affirmative action. NOW advocates equality for military servicewomen and favors allowing women to serve in combat roles. The organization publishes the quarterly *National NOW Times.*

National Partnership for Women & Families

1875 Connecticut Ave. NW, Suite 650, Washington, DC 20009
(202) 986-2600 • fax: (202) 986-2539
e-mail: info@nationalpartnership.org
Web site: www.nationalpartnership.org

The National Partnership for Women & Families is a nonprofit, nonpartisan organization that uses public education and advocacy to promote fairness in the workplace, quality health care, and policies that help men and women meet the demands of work and family. Its monthly newsletter, reports, and press releases are available for viewing on its Web site.

9to5 National Association of Working Women

152 W. Wisconsin Ave., Suite 408, Milwaukee, WI 53203
(414) 274-0925 • toll free: (800) 522-0925 • fax: (414) 272-2870
e-mail: 9to5@9to5.org • Web site: www.9to5.org

The organization seeks to gain better pay, opportunities for advancement, elimination of sex and race discrimination, and improved working conditions for female office workers. It publishes the *9to5 Newsletter* five times a year as well as numerous pamphlets.

Status of Women Canada (SWC)

MacDonald Bldg., 123 Slater St., 10th Fl., Ottawa, ON K1P 1H9 Canada
(613) 995-7835 • fax: (613) 957-3359
e-mail: information@swc-cfc.gc.ca • Web site: www.swc-cfc.gc.ca

Status of Women Canada is a federal government agency that promotes gender equality and the full participation of women in the economic, social, cultural, and political life of the country. SWC publishes the quarterly newsletter *Perspectives* and numerous reports, including "Economic Gender Equality Indicators" and "Round Table Report on the Portrayal of Young Women in the Media."

Wider Opportunities for Women (WOW)
1001 Connecticut Ave. NW, Suite 930, Washington, DC 20036
(202) 464-1596 • fax: (202) 464-1660
e-mail: info@wowonline.org • Web site: www.wowonline.org

WOW works to expand employment opportunities for women by overcoming sex-stereotypic education and training, work segregation, and discrimination in employment practices and wages. In addition to pamphlets and fact sheets, WOW publishes the book *A More Promising Future: Strategies to Improve the Workplace* and the quarterly newsletter *Women at Work.*

Women Work! The National Network for Women's Employment
1625 K St. NW, Suite 300, Washington, DC 20006
(202) 467-6346 • fax: (202) 467-5366
e-mail: womenwork@womenwork.org
Web site: www.womenwork.org

Women Work! fosters the development of programs and services that prepare women for the workforce. It acts as a clearinghouse, providing the public with technical assistance, training, information, data collection, legislative monitoring, and other services. It also provides referrals and information on research in progress and available programs. Women Work! develops and publishes a range of materials, including program curricula, legislative guides, statistical reports, and the quarterly newsletter *Network News.*

Bibliography of Books

Susan Shapiro Barash   *The New Wife: The Evolving Role of the American Wife.* Lenexa, KS: Nonetheless, 2004.

Simon Baron-Cohen   *The Essential Difference: The Truth About the Male and Female Brain.* Boulder, CO: Perseus, 2003.

John P. Bartkowski   *The Promise Keepers: Servants, Soldiers, and Godly Men.* Piscataway, NJ: Rutgers University Press, 2004.

Susan Bordo   *Unbearable Weight: Feminism, Western Culture, and the Body.* Berkeley and Los Angeles: University of California Press, 2004.

John Bridges   *How to Be a Gentleman: A Contemporary Guide to Common Courtesy.* Nashville, TN: Rutledge Hill, 2001.

Patrick Califia   *Sex Changes: Transgender Politics.* San Francisco: Cleis, 2003.

Maria Charles and David B. Grusky   *Occupational Ghettos: The Worldwide Segregation of Women and Men.* Stanford, CA: Stanford University Press, 2003.

Frances Cleaver   *Masculinities Matter! Men, Gender, and Development.* London: Zed, 2003.

John Colapinto   *As Nature Made Him: The Boy Who Was Raised as a Girl.* New York: HarperPerennial, 2001.

Ann Crittenden   *The Price of Motherhood: Why the Most Important Job in the World Is Still the Least Valued.* New York: Metropolitan, 2001.

Danielle Crittenden   *What Our Mothers Didn't Tell Us: Why Happiness Eludes the Modern Woman.* New York: Simon & Schuster, 1999.

Judith C. Daniluk   *Women's Sexuality Across the Life Span: Challenging Myths, Creating Meanings.* New York: Guilford, 2003.

Rory Dicker and Alison Piepmeier   *Catching a Wave: Feminism for the 21st Century.* Boston: Northeastern University Press, 2003.

Susan Douglas and Meredith Michaels   *The Mommy Myth: The Idealization of Motherhood and How It Has Undermined Women.* New York: Free Press, 2004.

Nancy E. Dowd   *Redefining Fatherhood.* New York: New York University Press, 2000.

Susan Faludi   *Stiffed: The Betrayal of the American Man.* New York: William Morrow, 1999.

Bill and Pam Farrel	*Why Men and Women Act the Way They Do: The Reasons Might Surprise You.* Eugene, OR: Harvest House, 2003.
Warren Farrell	*The Myth of Male Power.* New York: Penguin, 2001.
Anne Fausto-Sterling	*Sexing the Body: Gender Politics and the Construction of Sexuality.* New York: Basic Books, 2000.
Anna Fels	*Necessary Dreams: The Vital Role of Ambition in Women's Lives.* New York: Pantheon, 2004.
Marianne A. Ferber and Julie A. Nelson, eds.	*Feminist Economics Today: Beyond Economic Man.* Chicago: University of Chicago Press, 2002.
Carol L. Flinders	*Rebalancing the World: Why Women Belong and Men Compete and How to Restore the Ancient Equilibrium.* San Francisco: HarperSanFrancisco, 2003.
Susan Fraiman	*Cool Men and the Second Sex.* New York: Columbia University Press, 2003.
David D. Gilmore	*Misogyny: The Male Malady.* Philadelphia: University of Pennsylvania Press, 2001.
Joshua S. Goldstein	*War and Gender: How Gender Shapes the War System and Vice Versa.* New York: Cambridge University Press, 2003.
Marnina Gonick	*Between Femininities: Ambivalence, Identities, and the Education of Girls.* Albany: State University of New York Press, 2003.
Suzanne E. Hatty	*Masculinities, Violence, and Culture.* Thousand Oaks, CA: Sage Publications, 2000.
T. Walter Herbert	*Sexual Violence and American Manhood.* Cambridge, MA: Harvard University Press, 2002.
Barbara Hobson, ed.	*Making Men into Fathers: Men, Masculinities, and the Social Politics of Fatherhood.* New York: Cambridge University Press, 2002.
Ronald Inglehart and Pippa Norris	*Rising Tide: Gender Inequality and Cultural Change Around the World.* New York: Cambridge University Press, 2003.
Gisela Kaplan and Lesley J. Rogers	*Gene Worship: Moving Beyond the Nature/Nurture Debate over Genes, Brain, and Gender.* New York: Other, 2003.
Loretta E. Kaufman and Mary W. Quigley	*And What Do You Do? When Women Choose to Stay Home.* Berkeley, CA: Wildcat Canyon, 2003.
Michael S. Kimmel	*The Gendered Society.* New York: Oxford University Press, 2000.

Bobbi S. Low — *Why Sex Matters: A Darwinian Look at Human Behavior.* Princeton, NJ: Princeton University Press, 2000.

Deena Mandell — *Deadbeat Dads: Subjectivity and Social Construction.* Toronto: University of Toronto Press, 2002.

Sam Martin — *How to Mow the Lawn: The Lost Art of Being a Man.* New York: Dutton, 2003.

Anne Moir and Bill Moir — *Why Men Don't Iron: The Fascinating and Unalterable Differences Between Men and Women.* New York: Birch Lane, 2000.

Isabelle Muhlnickel — *Beleaguered American Males.* Bloomington, IN: 1st Books, 2000.

Tracie O'Keefe and Katrina Fox, eds. — *Finding the Real Me: True Tales of Sex and Gender Diversity.* San Francisco: Jossey-Bass, 2003.

Peggy J. Rudd — *Crossdressing with Dignity: The Case for Transcending Gender Lines.* Katy, TX: PM, 2003.

Lloyd E. Sandelands — *Male and Female in Social Life.* New Brunswick, NJ: Transaction, 2001.

Wendy Shalit — *A Return to Modesty: Discovering the Lost Virtue.* New York: Touchstone, 2000.

Christina Hoff Sommers — *The War Against Boys: How Misguided Feminism Is Harming Our Young Men.* New York: Touchstone, 2001.

Warren Steinberg — *Masculinity: Identity, Conflict, and Transformation.* Boston: Shambhala, 2001.

Jeannie Banks Thomas — *Naked Barbies, Warrior Joes, and Other Forms of Visible Gender.* Champaign: University of Illinois Press, 2003.

Lionel Tiger — *The Decline of Males.* New York: Golden Books, 1999.

John Townsend — *What Women Want—What Men Want: Why the Sexes Still See Love and Commitment So Differently.* New York: Oxford University Press, 1998.

Emily White — *Fast Girls: Teenage Tribes and the Myth of the Slut.* New York: Berkley, 2003.

Stephen Whitehead — *Men, Women, Love, and Romance: Under the Covers of the Bedroom Revolution.* London: Vision Paperbacks, 2003.

Joan Williams — *Unbending Gender: Why Family and Work Conflict and What to Do About It.* New York: Oxford University Press, 2001.

Naomi Wolf — *The Beauty Myth: How Images of Beauty Are Used Against Women.* New York: HarperPerennial, 2002.

Index

negative impact of, 118, 143–44
are not essential, 110–11, 119
biological sex differences and, 120–22
essentialist paradigm on, 118
feminism on, 111
importance of male role model and, 123–24
losing a father, 115–16
paternity leave for, 174
relationship with children, 113–15, 159
  father-daughter relationship, 24–26, 110
  father-son relationship, 25, 33
research on, 118
responsibilities of, 112
shared names and, 112–13
Fausto-Sterling, Anne, 38, 50, 52–53, 56, 57
Feinberg, Leslie, 45–46
females
  appeal of male power to, 161
  "bashing," 197–203
  as breadwinners, 160
  circumcision of, 33–36
  cultural variations on defining, 29–33
  have not taken men's jobs, 133
  have not used up all of health care, 133–34
  independence of
    dangers of dependency and, 79–80
    drawbacks of, 80–81, 82–83
    selfish heroine and, 78–79
  interests of, 23–24
  in the military, 62–63
  of New Guinea tribe, 31–32
  as nurturers, 163–64
  as peacemakers, 165
  reasons of, for divorce, 164–65, 166
  reduced earnings by, 170–71
  reproductive strategy of, 127–28
  in the school system, 19–20
  sexuality of, 163
  in sports, 24–25
  as submissive, 24
  see also male-female relationships; mothers/motherhood
Feminine Mystique (Friedan), 168–69
feminism/feminists
  benefits from, 99
  blame and criticism placed on, 88,

100–101, 201
  current threats to women's rights and, 103–104
  "dad-bashing" and, 111
  damaging effects of, 95–97, 138–41, 144–46
  as demeaning femininity, 95
  do not hate men, 150
  eradication of masculinity by, 133–34, 141
  has not robbed women of their birthright, 87–88
  has offered choices to men and women, 152–53
  impact of, on educational system, 142
  "lite," 103
  loss of respect for women due to, 93–94
  males demonized by, 139–40
  on marriage, 95
    desire for egalitarian, 171–76
  in early women's movement, 168
  equality and, 160–61
  religious right's and, 168
  during sixties movement, 168–69
  on men's power in the home, 159–60
  in the nineties, 186
  political correctness and, 101–103
  pornography war and, 103
  reluctance of women to identify with, 101
  as strong, 102
  on women's sexuality, 89
ferms (female pseudohermaphrodites), 39
financial/economic issues
  dual-income families and, 134–35
  female dominance and, 160–61
  men's power in the home and, 160
  stay-at-home mothers and, 66, 69
  working mothers and, 74, 90–91
fishing, 24
five-gender system, 39–41
French, Nicci, 147
Friedan, Betty, 168–69
Furchgott-Roth, Diana, 104

Gallese, Liz, 160
Gardner, Marilyn, 70
gay/lesbian parenting, 119, 123
gender
  cultural attitudes and, 28, 29–32, 33–36

as a divine creation, 55
flexibility, 135
problems with, 43–44
sex vs., 41
genitalia
  circumcision and, 32–36
  complete androgen insensitivity
    syndrome and, 53–54
  cultural vs. physical, 47–48
  intersexual marriages and, 46–47
  vaginal agenesis and, 57
Gino, Alex, 41
Glasson, Karl, 137
Goldberg, Bernard, 94
Goldberg, Jonah, 185
Gornick, Janet C., 167
Gottman, John, 166
Gray, John, 16
Green, Michael, 19
Greer, Germaine, 111–12

health care, 133–34
hemicastration, 33
herms (hermaphrodites), 39
Hijras, the (Native American tribe),
  44
homosexuality, 46, 47
hormone differences, 14–15
Horn, Wade, 104
Hume, David, 182
hunting, 24

infants, differences in care of, 16
infibulation, 34
International Bill of Gender Rights,
  46
intersexuality
  current approaches to management
    of, 40
  defining, 52–53, 55
  examples of, 44
  incidences of, 57–58
  legal/discriminatory challenges
    and, 45–46
  marriage and, 46–47
  medical treatment and, 40, 41–42
  natural/normal distinction and,
    58–59
  not focusing on genitalia and,
    44–45
  utopian vision on, 47–48

Jensen, Robert, 150

Karaim, Reed, 72

Kass, Amy, 156–57
Kennedy, Kate, 107
Kessler, Suzanne, 44–45
Kimmel, Michael S., 27, 135
Kirkland, Resa LaRu, 92
Klinefelter syndrome, 56

Lamb, M.E., 124
late-onset congenital adrenal
  hyperplasia, 54–56
Lynch, Jessica, 62
Lytton, H., 124

Mailer, Norman, 148
male-female relationships
  return to courtship and, 156–57
  strains in, 16
  traditional dating methods and,
    188–89
  see also marriage; modesty
males
  are poor mates, 128
  are shafted by the legal system,
    142–43
  "bashing of," 193, 194–95
    by feminists, 139–40
    con, 150
  blame placed on, 128–29
  circumcision of, 35
  college education of, vs. females,
    127–28
  commitment of, to
    marriage/family, 129–30
  commitment of, to work, 164
  cultural variations on defining,
    29–33
  divorce and, 123–24, 164–65
  as dominant, 24
  educational system is biased
    against, 141–42
    con, 19–20, 141–42
  interests of, 24–25
  masculinity of, 149–51
  need of, for isolation, 162–63
  negative media portrayals of,
    107–108
  as the new victims, 193–94
  as principle breadwinners, 169–70
  public education campaigns for,
    174–75
  rejection of worthwhile values by,
    140–41
  relations among, 127
  respect for women by, 93–94
  see also fathers/fatherhood